The Death of HMS *Goodall*. (HMS *Honeysuckle* coming alongside). *From a painting by Len Mobbs.*

LAST
BUT NOT LEAST

HMS *Goodall*,
torpedoed 29th April 1945

THE SURVIVORS
AND THEIR RESCUERS

Jackie thanks for you help

Vic Ould

Vic Ould

ARCTURUS PRESS

2004

ISBN 0 907322 93 X

Published by

ARCTURUS PRESS
The Manse : Fleet Hargate : Lincolnshire PE12 8LL
England

01406 423971 :
Fax 01406 422191

2004

Contents

Illustrations & Maps

Cover design by Guy Erwood. Original photographer unknown.

Acknowledgements

My grateful thanks to all who have sent accounts of their experiences in the *Goodall* disaster, very often with additional copies of reports and photographs; to Jackie Smith, for research and records; to Len Heydock of HMS Cotton; and to the Naval Branch of the Ministry of Defence, London; and finally to Peter Erwood of Arcturus Press, the publishers of this account. Throughout the preparation of this book my wife Pat has given invaluable help by her knowledge of computers and the Internet.

Without the assistance of all the above this book would not have been possible. I hope I have not missed anyone out, but if so, I offer my most sincere apologies.

Vic Ould
October 2004

Introduction

HMS *Goodall* holds the melancholy distinction of being the last ship of the Royal Navy to have been sunk in the European theatre of war during World War II. She met her fate at 1930hrs on Sunday 29th April 1945 when she was torpedoed in the Barents Sea by U-968, while acting as one of the escort vessels for Convoy RA66 homeward bound from Murmansk.

Many of the 98 who died were volunteers of 18 years of age or thereabouts, boys doing a man's job. The injured, a few of whom are still alive today, continue to suffer from the effects of that terrible event. Not for them the clouding of memories over the course of time; even now, over fifty years on, it was not easy to persuade them that these memories needed to be recorded for the sake of history. There were several of the survivors who, no matter how hard I tried, found it impossible to talk about and re-live their terrible experience. Several have since 'crossed the bar' and with them have died their recollections of that fateful day.

In those distant times there was no such thing as counselling, the treatment of survivors usually consisting of a few days 'Survivor's Leave' and then swift drafting to another ship. After all, survivors were now experienced personnel, and it might even have been considered a bad influence on general morale to have survivors 'kicking around' in barracks for any length of time, perhaps demoralizing other ratings awaiting drafts to ships. Whatever the truth of the matter, survivors never stayed long in barracks.

The irony of this particularly tragic story is that the convoy with its remaining escorts arrived back in UK in time for the celebrations of VE day; but there was little to celebrate for the families and friends of those lost in *Goodall*. They would have known nothing until that dreaded telegram arrived which started 'We regret to inform you....' This was the fear that many at home who had loved ones in the Forces lived with. Even the 'missing believed killed' held out a slender hope, but the possibility of survival in the cold waters of the Kola Inlet was measured more in minutes than in hours. There would be no public announcement made at the time a ship was lost, which was looked upon as giving information to the enemy and perhaps lowering public morale. After a period of time casualty lists would be released and would appear in *The Times* newspaper. It was six weeks after *Goodall* was sunk that the casualty list appeared. Not everybody was aware of this system and of course not everybody read *The Times* anyway.

Designated 'next of kin' were recorded on the sailor's personal record and in his pay/identity book as 'Mother', 'Wife' or whatever, but nobody else would be informed. There must have been many a girl left wondering why her boyfriend went back to his ship promising faithfully to write and nothing was heard from him again. Unless she lived near him and knew his home, she would only know his address as 'HMS *Goodall*, c/o GPO London'.

What of the survivors themselves? Even those who had not been physically injured lost so much, even the clothes they had been wearing. Heavy seaboots had to be kicked off as soon as they hit the water or they would quickly drag you down. Bell-bottom trousers were so designed as to be discarded in this situation to give a chance of swimming, but they were still not that easy to remove when wet. They had lost many of their shipmates. On a small ship one knew every face even if you did not know the name to go with it; they had probably seen their 'oppos' (best mates) killed, injured or swept away from them. All their personal belongings, photographs and letters along with addresses, presents they may have bought to take home and any money they had. Their 'Tiddley Suits', ie, their very best uniform tailor-made ashore and costing a lot of pay, worn especially for home leave, something they would have difficulty claiming for. Gone was their ship, but it was not just a ship, it was their home and they were part of her twenty four hours a day, every day except for the few occasions when leave was granted. Like their 'Tiddley Suits', their ship was something to be proud of. Even though she heaved, rolled and made you as sick as a dog, it was still your home. When at sea it was cold, wet, and uncomfortable, with condensation running down the bulkheads so the messdecks were often wet underfoot; but with all the problems you were proud of your ship. When it was no longer there, it must have been a deeply depressing time.

True to all the traditions of the Royal Navy, HMS *Goodall* in her role as an escort charged with the safekeeping of her convoy knew the risks and did not hesitate. She went in to attack and according to the records she passed the signal 338. 20. 'Sub definite', when the torpedo explosion at 1935 hrs cut short the remainder of the message. In a matter of minutes she was a mass of flames, with many dead, injured and others fighting to survive. A scene terrible enough even for the other ships in company to witness, let alone those who were aboard the stricken vessel herself.

So, when readers come to the end of this book of eye-witness recollections of that fateful day, there should be no doubt in their minds that HMS *Goodall* was LAST BUT NOT LEAST.

HMS *Goodall* was a 'Captain' Class frigate of the EVART type (Diesel-Electric short-hulled Destroyer Escort).

Overall Length 289ft,
Beam 35ft.
Machinery: 6000 BHP Diesel-Electric, two shafts.
Range: 6000 nautical miles at 12 knots.
Armament: Three x 3-inch guns, plus Oerlikon 20mm cannon.
The number of Oerlikons fitted was increased over the ship's lifetime, with something like 20 having been installed by the time she was sunk.
The quantity of depth charges carried was also increased and in the end she had about 160 depth-charges and also 'Hedgehog' anti-submarine mortars.
Commissioned 4th October 1943.
Commanding Officer: Lt-Cdr J.V. FULTON RNVR.
Pennant Number K479.
She was named after Samuel Granston Goodall who commanded HMS Defiance at the Battle of Ushant in 1778.
Her Battle Honours were: Atlantic 1944 : Arctic 1945.

Roll of Honour

Temp. Sub/Lt	J.D.Armstrong	RNVR.
A/Lt. Cdr.	J.V.Fulton	RNVR.
Temp. A/Gunner	Mr.H. Gravil	RN.
Temp. Sub/Lt.	G.N.Horspool	RNZVR.
Temp. Lt.	R.R.Whyte	RNVR.

Abraham, Frederick C	A/B	C/JX 105759.
Ainsworth, Ronald	Signalman	C/JX 573356.
Barry, Frederick B	Actg A/B	C/JX 319813.
Bourne, Ronald J	A/B	C/JX 639081.
Bryant, George W	P/O Stoker	C/KX 83388.
Callaghan, James C	A/B	C/JX 654142.
Campbell, James	Actg A/B	C/JX 656307.
Carter, George	Stoker 1st Class	C/KX 122509.
Clark, Dennis W.C	Ord/Seaman	C/JX 316778.
Clarke, Joseph	Ldg Seaman (Ty)	C/JX 308037.
Cobb, Bernard J.C	Tel. (S)	C/JX 405703.
Cole, Terence F	Stoker 1st Class	C/KX 143641.
Collins, Ronald F	Actg ERA 4th Class	C/MX 119444.
Collyer, Dudley R	Ldg Stores Ass.(Ty)	C/MX 85584.
Copeland, Arnold	Actg A/B	C/JX 625957.
Cowper, John B	A/B	C/JX 391733.
Culpan, Frank R	Actg A/B	C/JX 664536.
Cumberpatch, Owen D	A/B	C/JX 408071.
Daniel, Thomas A	Tel (S)	C/JX 405711.
Day, Joseph	A/B	C/JX 192773.
Emsley, Donald W	Ord/Seaman	C/JX 702969.
Ffitch, Stanley W	Steward	C/LX 571253.
Finlay, George	Actg P/O Tel.(Ty)	C/J 229160.
Forrest, Alan W	A/B	C/JX 638755.
Fry, Herbert H.C	Signalman	C/JX 616247.
Gardiner, William C	A/B	C/JX 315322.
Gill, Stanley J	A/B	C/JX 319336.
Gundy, Wilfred J	Actg P/O Radio Mech	P/MX 575794.
Hall, Albert	Actg A/B	C/JX 548000.
Hall, John	Actg A/B	C/Jx 555833.
Hamilton, Thomas	A/B	C/JX 206276.
Harling, Harry	Actg Stoker 1st Class	C/KX 141970.

Hibbert, Sam	Actg A/B	C/JX 317982.
Holland, Harry A	A/B	C/JX 151489.
Howkins, Fred	Stoker 1st Class	C/KX 140449.
Jackson, Arthur	Coder	C/JX 508890.
Jeffries, Douglas	Actg L/Seaman (Ty)	C/SSX 33199.
Jennings, John J	A/B	C/JX 391800.
Jones, Percival E	A/B	C/JX 271640.
Kayes, Gordon K	A/B	C/JX 337420.
Kelly, James G	A/B	C/JX 549026.
Kemp, Dick	Stoker 1st Class	C/KX 127417.
Keyes, Norman W.C	A/B	C/JX 678194.
Kipling, Thomas H	A/B	C/JX 549738.
Laws, James A	L/Seaman (RFR)	C/J 113444.
McCusker, James	Actg A/B	C/JX 352042.
McNicholl, Richard	Ldg/Cook (S) (Ty)	C/MX 574190.
Marshall, George	Act L/Stoker (Ty)	C/KX 107888.
Mason, Ernest A	Ldg/Cook (Ty)	C/MX 94088.
Mawson, Raymond	Telelegraphist	C/JX 387319.
Millen, Harold L	P/O Tel (RFR)	C/J 106312.
Miller, Charles Mckay	Stoker 1st Class	C/KX 85266.
Mills, Gordon	Actg Stoker 1st Class	C/KX 141501.
Murphy, Albert	Stoker 1st Class	C/KX 129806.
Osborne, Frederick A	Stoker 1st Class	C/KX 103609.
Palmer, Cyril P	A/B	C/JX 548865.
Pearce, Alexander G	Actg L/Seaman (Ty)	C/JX 352080.
Pedersen, Jens H.S	Asst Steward	C/LX 645358.
Pope, Charles R.J	Telegraphist	C/JX 577277.
Pulford, Walter	A/B	C/JX 300741.
Rawlinson, John E	Actg L/Signalman (Ty)	C/JX 250245.
Reid, James	Actg L/Stoker (Ty)	C/KX 130760.
Reid, William G	Actg Eng Room Art 4th Class	C/MX 92964.
Rodwell, Peter J	Ldg Stoker (Ty)	C/KX 104759.
Ronnie, Norman	A/B	C/JX 659044.
Rooke, Thomas	Ordnance/Art 3/Class	C/SR 8801.
Routley, Henry J	A/B	C/JX 551927.
Sivell, Sidney W.G	Signalman	C/JX 515247.
Smith, Albert E	Ord/Seaman	C/JX 540092.
Smith, Donald O	Stoker 1st Class	C/KX 110962.
Smith, Frederick H	A/B	C/JX 542259.
Smith, Leslie B	A/B	C/JX 547856.
Smith, Stanley W	Ord/Seaman	C/JX 721350.

Smith, William L	A/B	C/JX 557060.
Sparkes, Fred S	Ord/Telegraphist	C/JX 371503.
Stanners, Alexander S M	A/B	C/JX 454828.
Steadman, Cyril D	Ldg Seaman	D/JX 214913.
Stonehouse, Cyril	P/O	C/J 108065.
Swankie, Joseph T	A/B	C/JX 353265.
Swinbourne, Edward W.J	Ord/ Seaman	C/JX 538664.
Thurbin, Arthur	Stoker 1st Class	C/KX 156181.
Timms, John C	A/B	C/JX 566994.
Tuck, Sidney H	A/B	C/JX 294780.
Tuckley, Cranley W.T	A/B	C/JX 399935.
Wakelin, Arthur M	Actg P/O (Ty)	C/SSX 32875.
Ward, Joseph	A/B	C/JX 397886.
Warren, Lael	Elec Art 4th Class	C/MX 118371.
Willcocks, Samuel J	Ldg Seaman (Ty)	C/SSX 16965.
Williams, Guy E	Coder	C/JX 230263.
Wilson, Richard B	P/O Steward (Ty)	C/LX 22170.

Died of wounds

Dowles, Walter F	A/B	C/JX 184993.
Quinby, Wilfred R	Stoker 1st Class	C/KX 145575.
Shotton, William	Actg ERA 4th Class	C/MX 97862.

Other casualties

The two members of the seaboat's crew who died when it capsized in the rescue of survivors from the sinking of HMS *Bullen* were:

Sills, Herbert	Ord/Seaman	D/JX 650891.
Whittick, Stanley	A/B	C/JX 308324.

One other of HMS *Goodall*'s crew was killed on 14.12.1944:

Herbert, Harry	Ord/Seaman	C/JX 566996.

He was on home leave in London and both he and his wife Mildred died at home in Southgate when the area was hit by an enemy V2 rocket.

NOTE: In instances where different sources have been researched, personal details on records have varied. Where uncertainty remained, the information on the Commonwealth War Graves Commission's website (www.cwgc.org) has been used.

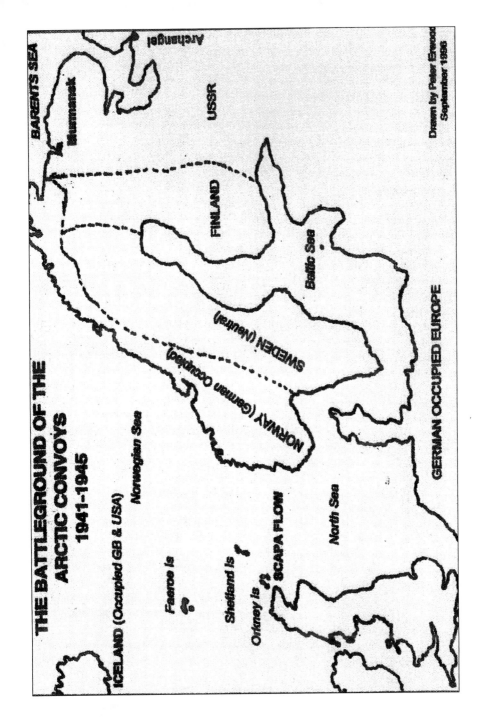

THE BATTLEGROUND OF THE
ARCTIC CONVOYS
1941-1945

ICELAND (Occupied GB & USA)

Norwegian Sea

Faeroe Is

Shetland Is

Orkney Is

SCAPA FLOW

North Sea

BARENTS SEA

Archangel

Murmansk

USSR

FINLAND

Baltic Sea

SWEDEN (Neutral)

NORWAY (German Occupied)

GERMAN OCCUPIED EUROPE

Drawn by Peter Elwood
September 1996

7

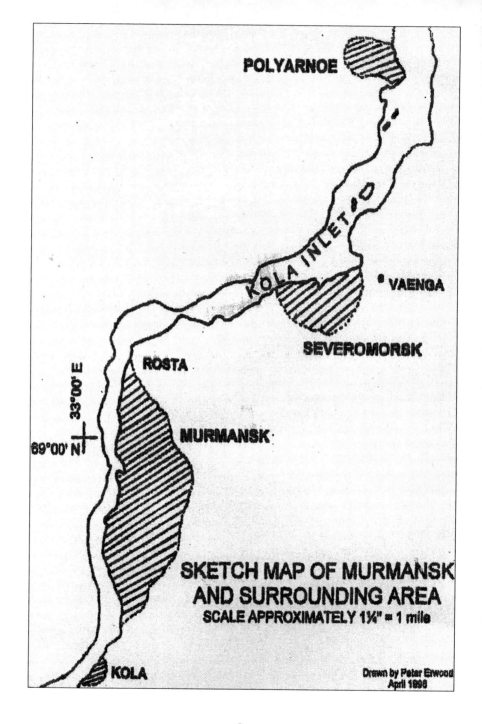

POLYARNOE

KOLA INLET

VAENGA

SEVEROMORSK

ROSTA

33°00' E

69°00' N

MURMANSK

KOLA

SKETCH MAP OF MURMANSK
AND SURROUNDING AREA
SCALE APPROXIMATELY 1¼" = 1 mile

Drawn by Peter Elwood
April 1996

8

All in a day's work

The following log is a report of one of the early assignments carried out by HMS *Goodall* and provides a typical picture of experiences by convoys and their escorts in general. Note this was January 1944 and *Goodall* had only been completed and commissioned the previous October. Not a great deal of time for any ship's company to become fully experienced, especially when you take into account that many had only been in the RN for a short time and in many cases not even been to sea previously.

Report 15 January 1944

HMS *Goodall* (Senior Officer) in company with HMS *Aylmer* sailed from Argentia Newfoundland at 1705 hrs on 3rd. Jan.1944 with orders to catch up B2 Group which had sailed also from the same port at 1830 hrs the previous day. The two ships were to be additional escorts for Convoy HX 273 to UK.

Difficulties were encountered even meeting up with the convoy because during the night of 4th/5th January North/North West winds caused speed to be reduced to 11 knots and these winds further increased to full gale strength causing a further reduction to 6 knots two hours later. At this speed the two ships were not only at the mercy of the weather but could also have been in dire trouble from any lurking U-Boats. Radar detection giving 'echoes' on the screen at 15-20 miles were presumed to be the convoy which was also suffering badly from the storm, with ships scattered and out of their positions. *Goodall* set course to pass astern of the convoy and come up on the starboard side to take up station; the USS *David Bushnell* was overtaken and ordered to take station astern.

On 6th January HMS *Aylmer* was sent as the result of Radar contact to bring in USS *Thomas Heyward*, the visibility at the time being 1 - 2 miles. At this point results from the homing procedure put the convoy approximately 25 miles ahead and *Aylmer* was sent on to contact the convoy by Radar and to pass *Goodall*'s position to S/O B2 group. The 7th January brought the starboard quarter of the convoy to about 7 miles away, but during that night the range opened to 17 miles owing to an error in the compass of USS *David Bushnell*. The compass on *Goodall* had already broken down on the night of 4th January when the storm had caused excessive rolling of the ship and much mercury in the compass had been lost, leaving it defective for the remainder of the voyage.

On 8th January Radar reported an echo on the starboard quarter of the convoy at 30 miles range. *Goodall* was ordered to intercept, and the echo was found to be from USS *Samuel Moody*, which was ordered to join *Goodall*. The three US ships were then escorted to the remainder of the convoy 10 miles away and at 1552 hrs. had safely rejoined the convoy.

On 10th January *Goodall*, *Aylmer* and *Bentley*, with *Balfour* in command were detached by S/O B2 Group from the convoy HX 273 to act as an independent unit and carry out an offensive anti-submarine and radar sweep, a report having been received that the convoy had been sighted by U-boats. A contact was made on 11th January by *Balfour*, but on investigation proved to be 'non-sub'. Then at 0335 hrs a signal was intercepted from HMS *Mourne* indicating an HF/DF bearing of a U-boat 095 degrees range 10 miles from her. Area was searched but no contact was made so patrol was resumed until 1100 hrs when course was altered to join the convoy ON 219 as orders had been received to act as additional escorts to support this convoy.

The weather at this time was not good, wind force 7 south east by east with heavy rain and the maximum visibility two miles. At 1650 hrs on 11th Jan. contact was made with the convoy ON 219 proceeding on the reciprocal course and speed was adjusted to suit. The four frigates then remained at their allotted positions until 12th January, when *Balfour* was forced to leave, having reached her prudent limit of endurance. Then at 2355 hrs *Goodall* in company with *Bentley* and *Aylmer* were instructed to leave convoy ON 219 to carry out an anti-submarine sweep with the co-operation of an aircraft (Liberator). The search went on until 2310 hrs on 13th Jan with no U-boat contact being made. The ships then set sail for Bangor with the group, arriving off New Island at 1100 hrs on 15th Jan.

During the day of the 13th large amounts of water noise on *Goodall* gave reason to suspect that the Asdic dome was punctured, which was later confirmed. The only incident otherwise for the group occurred at 1947 hrs on 14th Jan when course had to be altered to avoid a USN Task Force consisting of 12 destroyers and sundry other vessels.

Reports on the loss of HMS Goodall

By Lieutenant J.S. Dallaway, RN and

Chief Stoker Alfred W. Lawrence C/K65242

Report of Lieutenant J S Dallaway RN
First Lieutenant of HMS Goodall *and Senior Officer surviving.*

To HMS Vindex
Sir.

(1) I have the honour to submit the following report on the circumstances attending the loss of His Majesty's Ship *Goodall* by enemy action off Kola Inlet, North Russia on Sunday 29th. April 1945.

(2) The ship was steaming in a northerly direction with HMS *Anguilla* stationed approximately one mile to starboard carrying out independant 'zig-zag', speed of ship was 12 knots and unifoxer streamed.

The ship's company were closed up at 'undersea action stations'.

(3) When about 15 minutes after the first U-boat had been surfaced and sunk by gunfire at 1904 hrs. HMS *Goodall* gained a contact and reduced speed to attacking speed, 'hedgehog' crew standing by. The order was passed through the a/s intercom to standby 'hedgehog' at about 1925 hrs and at about 1930 hrs the ship was struck either by a mine or torpedo resulting in a violent explosion due to the 3-inch magazine of A and B guns being hit. My action station was aft with the depth-charge crew at X gun and the first indication I had that we had been hit was that I found myself stretched out on deck with debris falling all around, the ship settling fast forward and listing to starboard.

(4) Having got to my feet I took a hasty look around and realised that the forward section of the ship from the break in the forecastle was completely missing. The bridge had been turned right over, falling onto the funnel, midship Oerlikon gun crews and supply parties, finally coming to rest hanging over the starboard side with the mainmast falling down on the deck portside.

(5) The Captain was on the bridge at this time and after the explosion no trace of him could be seen and I presumed he was lost and proceeded to act accordingly. Under the bridge, where the diesel

tanks were situated holding a full capacity of 80 tons, fire broke out; also the forward engine room was on fire. Soon the whole midship section was ablaze, enveloping the bridge. I asked the engineer if anything could be done about the fire; he told me nothing was working because all power had failed. The fire and the bridge blocked all our passages on board, which was further aggravated by the midship Oerlikon ready-to-use stowages exploding and the Oerlikon ammunition exploding all over the place.

(6) During this time engine room ratings, repair parties and depth charge crews had assembled aft, very quickly calmed down and obeyed my orders to clear away remaining rafts as the ship had taken a further list up to deck level from number two motor room forward. It was impossible to get either of the motorboats or the whaler down owing to structural damage.

(7) By this time I had lost all idea of time, the fire was gaining aft and I realised that it would not be long before it reached the after 3-inch ammunition and 'hedgehog' magazines for which the spraying system had failed as this was dependent on the main fire and flushing system. Owing to the large amount of ammunition which was stowed there I realized that with the fit hands available I could not hope to clear it, so I ordered the men into the rafts and told them to get clear as the magazines were likely to blow up at any moment.

(8) Three rafts with about 15 to 20 men in each and one floatnet with 6 ratings started to get clear of the ship. The badly wounded and one officer were kept onboard laid out on the quarterdeck and on checking up I found that a total of 13 officers and men were left onboard. I explained the situation to them, that the magazines were in danger and all available rafts had left and told them to either jump for it and make their way to the rafts or remain whilst we cleared anything that would float, such as smoke floats etc. So, assisted by the engineer officer and other ratings prepared to make a raft from any pieces of timber we could gather such as the ensign staff, dan buoy spars to which we attached tail lines for lashing the weak and wounded.

The ship, during this time fortunately drifted so that she lay beam to wind and sea. I realized that the flames were now athwartships and the danger to the magazines had passed, so with the engineer officer and Able Seaman Gordon West C/JX 408320, we proceeded to check up the doors of the afterpart. I then told Able Seaman West and Able Seaman William Gillott C/JX 318663 to carry on and bring Able Seaman Goss who was discovered badly wounded in the after

Oerlikon gun position, as there was little else we could do by this time.

(9) Things became a little more comfortable and we settled down aft to await events. It was at this stage that the fuel oil caught fire about three hundred yards to starboard, and then HMS *Honeysuckle* was seen approaching and she laid alongside while the ratings struggled clear and boarded her.

We were completely exhausted by this time and it took three of us to drag Able Seaman Goss to the ship's side and as we did not have the strength to pass him over I bent a line around his waist, passed the other end of the line to HMS *Honeysuckle* and lowered him into the water. The other injured men under the charge of the engineer officer were also passed across.

(10) During this process a Sub-Lieutenant from *Honeysuckle* boarded the ship to give assistance, and pointed out to me that one rating was trapped in the bridge structure whom I failed to observe due to the fire and my full attention being absorbed by the ship's immediate needs.

This rating was Telegraphist Fenwick who at our shouting made his way down to the after Oerlikon gun position, and was assisted to the quarterdeck by the Sub-Lieutenant. I had to be quite firm with this Sub-Lieutenant, as he was quite prepared to pass through the fire and exploding ammunition, and I very reluctantly ordered him not to do so. When all the ratings were aboard HMS *Honeysuckle* there was nothing further that the engineer officer or myself could do. We left our ship and *Honeysuckle* proceeded to pick up men from the Carley floats and assist her boat which she had previously lowered while coming alongside. It was then seen that the floatnet was dangerously near to the oil fire and with extreme coolness the commanding officer of HMS *Honeysuckle* proceeded to rescue these men. As the last of these ratings was being hauled aboard flames from the fire were sweeping the port side of the ship.

(11) When HMS *Honeysuckle* had drawn clear of the fire I reported to her Captain that the after part of HMS *Goodall* was tight and dry; and if towing the wreck was contemplated the engineer officer and myself with a few ratings were quite prepared to go back on board. His reply was that the matter was out of his hands and that *Honeysuckle* was rejoining the group.

(12) By this time Russian MTB's and *Farnham Castle* were on the scene and assisted in picking up men from the water. We then returned to harbour having a total of three officers and thirty-six

ratings.

Names and official numbers of all known survivors were passed to the SBNO North Russia, Polyarnoe by HM Ships *Honeysuckle* and *Farnham Castle*, both corvettes on escort duty, but I have reason to believe that some ratings may have been picked up by Russian M.T.B's who had not arrived in harbour by this time.

One officer and eight ratings were handed to RNAH Vaenga as cot cases; the remainder were transferred to HMS *Vindex*.

A nominal list of the officers and ratings accompanies this report. (13) The confidential books and signal publications were all kept in a big safe in the forward cabin, this whole structure was destroyed in the explosion and I therefore consider the risk of their compromise negligible.

Certain orders and secret documents in the Captain's 'sea pack' which when at sea he kept in his sea cabin with current S.P's for the use of the W/T and coding office would have been destroyed in the explosion or fire when the bridge structure was ablaze.

I cannot vouch for the destruction of these documents as they could have been flung into some odd corner. In this connection it is observed that all cypher books and tables were kept in the safe referred to as being destroyed, and that all cyphering was carried out in the forward cabin, and there is, therefore, no possibility of these books being compromised.

(14) In conclusion, I should like to place on record that the prompt action of the commanding officer of HMS *Honeysuckle* and his complete disregard of the danger of exploding ammunition whilst alongside, and the cool manner in which he took his ship right to the burning oil resulted in saving men from the floatnet and raft from being burnt alive and was worthy of the highest praise.

I should also like to strongly commend the behaviour of Able Seamen West and Gillott who assisted me in doing what we could for the ship, i/e checking doors, inspecting magazines, rescuing badly wounded etc. Both ratings showed complete disregard for their own personal safety throughout and stayed behind to assist wounded when they could have gone with the Carley floats.

(15) Brief statements taken from ratings whose evidence was thought to be of particular value are appended.

I have the honour to be, Sir,

      your obedient servant

                    James. S. Dallaway
                    Lieutenant, Royal Navy.

Chief Stoker Alfred W Lawrence C/K65242.
Appendix to the report on the loss of HMS Goodall.

I was standing outside the damage control headquarters when the explosion occurred. I saw debris falling and managed to dive clear into the damage control position, pushing the Engineer Officer with me. I helped him to his feet and asked him if he was alright and he replied 'Yes'. I then went over to the port side and went as far as the galley and found the door twisted. When I saw I could not do anything forward I came back amidships and ordered Able Seaman Gerald A Bently to go aft. By this time all the midship section was on fire and ammunition was exploding in all directions. I then helped Petty Officer V R Knighton C/SSX23691 to clear away the remaining rafts. The First Lieutenant then ordered the men into them and to get clear as the magazines were in danger. I helped Petty Officer Knighton to get the floatnet over and assisted the men into the rafts. When all rafts were manned and nothing further could be done, I took the last raft away obeying the order to abandon ship. While on the raft on the starboard side I was able to see the fire below the bridge which I think was the forward oil fuel tank. The whole forward section of the ship from below the bridge to the stem was completely missing. I do not think that anything other than what was done could have been done as all four mains were out of action and auxiliary fire appliances were damaged. While on the raft we overturned three times due to overcrowding and we were unable to clear the paddles as our hands were too numbed. I saw two men lost on the raft and we were eventually picked up by a boat from *Honeysuckle*. While going alongside HMS *Farnham Castle* we grabbed a line thrown from the ship, but due to the speed of the ship while she was drawing clear of the fire the boat turned over. We were then pulled inboard and only six survived. The time was 2045 as I saw the clock on the quarterdeck of HMS *Farnham Castle*.

HMS *Goodall* at Sea. A photo in possession of Mr David Parker, son-in-law of the late Bob Setchell.

Recollections of some survivors of *HMS* Goodall

W. Bates : H Carter : G. Cook : J. Dallaway : G Halliday :
W. Henderson ; F. James : S. Keeler : R. Knighton :
A. Lawrence : C. Lovitt ; P. Mallett : C. Martin : G. Mason :
F. Peeters : G. Roy : C. Russell : E.N. Setchell : R.B. Whyte

W (Bill) Bates Telegraphist

I joined *Goodall* direct from Boys Service early in 1944 and my first sight of her turned me into the proudest 'man' in the world. I had never seen a flush-deck Frigate before although I am told 'DE's' (Destroyer Escorts) did come up the Thames early in 1943. As I went aboard in the early hours her auxiliaries were mumbling and I felt her warmth that was far more than the galley could take credit for. The 'Boys' were cursing headaches from the night before, drinking huge mugs of steaming hot tea and scratching themselves back into consciousness in the time-honoured manner of all seamen. There were no greetings, just a gruff 'there's a mug there opps', then back to their yawning and scratching. All this languid manner was to belie what took place in the next half hour; she was then a 'tiddley' ship, smart, clean, wide-eyed and efficient. I must admit to feeling inadequate to meet their demanding standards but the 'lads' helped out and we sailed the next morning into a force nine and a bout of sea sickness that I shall remember all my life. I kept my 'watches', though, for those two horrendous days until blessed relief came and I was sick no more for the next four years. Our mess was situated below the Wardroom and 'Galley Flat' with a hatch leading to the forecastle break and on the starboard side a passage leading forward to the Stokers mess, heads and all the other sundry items of a forecastle compartment. Being compartmentalised I always felt an intuitive instinct to rap the bulkhead when going forward or aft. It was as if you were entering a neighbour's house; in reality the welcome from all messes was as if one was a long lost relative. It seemed strange at first to have the stokers forward and seamen aft, but on my many tours to the 'Laundry Flat' I got to know most of the 'lads'.

Yes, most found her a hard ship; she rolled and she corkscrewed in the mildest of weather and I believe one of our group noted a record 46-degree roll from port to starboard in two and a half seconds! Then of course, there was the welding, our Engineer showed us a bump we had 'picked up' when entering Gladstone Dock. From inside the engine room it was huge, but resting his back on a motor frame he put his foot on the bump and without much effort pushed it out.

What was it then that made the DE crews quite unique? Was it the fact that we were sailing in an American-built over-glamourised vessel in the way that our American cousins tended to and did we bask in the reflected, but unwarranted glory of it all? I think not. It has long been my belief that the crews that were sent to Boston US, to take over these ships were untrained, with over 70% of them having no sea time at all. In fact only one in four Officers had 'Watch Keeping' certificates! It was this reliance on each other during the initial period of 'Working Up' and the first convoys that made them such close knit crews. In all humility we bared our faults and no one was denied understanding to the common cause. Mistakes were a way of learning our craft and in doing so in a friendly rivalry showed our strengths and weaknesses. We didn't have the 'Pusser' ruggedness of the Fleet Destroyer or their crews and our very shape made us the 'Prima Donna's' of the sea, but it was us, with the Lochs and River Class that finally made the grade.

We received our orders and sailed for Kola on Friday the 13th April 1945. Many old hands were gratefully drafted off to go for their higher rates; it was therefore to be a tragic first and last journey for the new hands that came aboard. Convoy JW66 was shadowed by subs and aircraft from Bear Island during the last stages of the journey and 'Intelligence' informed us that U-Boats were converging on the area. We were closed up at Action Stations for most of the last few days, but I believe the group managed to keep the convoy safe from above and below. I have not heard of any ships being sunk or damaged on the outward leg.

After a desolate run ashore in Polyarnoe, the lads got to know that the local children were starving and, as many were in a very bad way we organised a large party of libertymen to smuggle some chocolate, grub and tickler ashore. Polyarnoe itself was flattened, but there was a path about three feet wide that one was allowed to tread (step off and you were menaced by a Rusky tommy-gunner). However, with so many of us we managed to slip the kids their treats and went back aboard very happy. Looking back on those few days in Polyarnoe I can't help but remember the comfort we shared on our messdecks in

18

comparison to the 'dug outs' and hovels the people ashore endured. We were fed well enough to be satisfied and with the blessing of warmth and good jovial mates life felt safe and cosy. On the upper deck and ashore life was bleak, grey and bitterly cold as if all the Novembers of history had gathered together to permeate one's soul with everlasting morbidity.

We sailed on the 29th April 1945 and encountered mines that had been laid by the U-Boats to drift into our path and cause confusion. In fact, despite the seriousness of the situation most of the hands on deck had a good laugh at the efforts of the gunners to sink the mines. The comfort of the harbour was still with us, it seemed.

My Action Station had been changed for the return journey, to the emergency wireless cubby amidships and when *Loch Insh* and *Goodall* made first contact with U-307 I had a privileged position to witness the action at first hand. This time there were no restrictions and provided I stayed within earshot of the speaker I could move around. Needless to say this 'promotion' and freedom was most welcomed and I was elated. *Loch Insh* brought U-307 to the surface and in the half light we witnessed her crew scrambling out of the conning tower. It was not until they brought their gun to bear on us that our skipper ordered 'open fire' with the Oerlikon. I can remember to this day the tracer hitting and ricocheting off the hull and conning tower and seeing men jumping desperately into the sea while others on their gun kept firing. We sheered off as she went down, but within seconds *Goodall* seemed to leap out of the water and come to a complete stop. I did not hear the explosion and as I tried to move I found that the door to the three foot square cubby had jammed and there was water and acid fumes filling up the space. There was no light and an effort to get my lifebelt torch to work proved useless. Despite frantic efforts to free the door I could not get out and finally with practically no air left and my eyes burning I got down as near as I could to the deck. I have no idea how long I was there, nor how or why at the time the door suddenly opened, I was grateful to be out of that coffin and free. There were bodies and parts of bodies laying all over the deck and hanging from the Oerlikon gun pit, one gunner minus his head was jammed between the gun shield and my Oppo lay just outside the door. As I tried to move him he seemed to come apart in my hands and I recall how ashamed I was to feel such revulsion. I made my way to the port side to go forward in an effort to get to the main wireless office, but as I got near to the break I saw the whole of the bridge superstructure had been blown

19

back abaft the funnel and the whole of the forecastle had disappeared from stem to aft of 'B' Gun. Fire was raging all around and ammo from ready-use lockers and magazines was exploding. I managed to climb under the smashed whaler and looked inside the Galley flat, but there and our mess below was just a mass of flames. 'Jimmy' (First Lieutenant) and the Engineer told us that the main magazine had gone but there were eighty tons of oil ready to blow and at this rate the fire would reach the other magazines within minutes. Those of us that were left climbed under the mast and rigging that had crashed onto the deck and made our way aft to the quarterdeck.

The wounded were laid out on the deck and the depth-charge crews began to defuse the charges. Regrettably that meant the remains of the masthead lookout and another unrecognizable man had to be sent over the side with it .Just about this time I heard a shout from the starboard side and saw a wounded rating on the deck by the after motor room hatch. A P/O and myself managed to crawl to him but fire and exploding ammo made us drag him along the deck to the first break in the depth-charge racks. Then two others joined us and we were ordered to take the wounded man over the side onto part of a floatnet. By this time the sea was on fire within a few yards of our position and I can remember my thoughts at that moment.

My 'Oppos' were in that blazing inferno where the wireless office used to be. Gone were the laughs and the catcalls, gone was the warm cosy mess deck and getting ready for a run ashore and what about old Finnegan's mum who needed him? It was as if I had come home to London again during the Blitz to find the house gone and all those precious moments that had gone into making a home had been taken away. There was a great empty space within me as I took hold of the wounded rating and went over the side. There was no fear, just a dull desolation and loneliness for the mates who fed the kids with me and showed me the ropes when I was a mere 'sprog'. God willing I hope they are having a run ashore in a much better place now.

The wounded rating died and drifted away sometime after we had been in the sea. It was far too cold to grasp the ropes of the floatnet so we wove our arms through the netting and hoped for the best. As we struggled to keep ahead of the flames we saw men who were on bits of Carley rafts drift into the flames and others who had jumped port side meet the blaze as the ship swung to port. We were no more than a few feet from the blazing oil for all the time we were in the sea, but as my lungs were already affected earlier by the acid fumes I must have passed out, because the next thing I was aware of was a rope lashing me across the face. I was dimly aware that I was now alone and voices were screaming, the whole world seemed to be in a red glow and as I turned my head I realized that a ship was just fifteen to twenty feet away. I could see her bows were actually in the flames and being unable to fashion a bowline, I wound the oily rope under my armpits and fearfully let go of the floatnet. As the lads pulled on the rope it slipped through my hands and I realized I had to roll over in an attempt to get another purchase. I just made the scrambling net when all my remaining strength left me but two lads from *Honeysuckle* came over the side and into the sea to pull all my six foot two and thirteen stone over the side. I can vaguely recall laying on the deck while fire and damage control parties rushed about their duties and I was listening to the battle that was taking place somewhere near. Then I was taken to a messdeck that was already smothered in oil and had the stench of smoke and vomit. My clothes were cut from me and I was made to swallow all sorts of emetics while the lads cleaned most of the oil away. It was then I realized why I was in so much pain from my lower abdomen down and I panicked and recalled that the depth charges that had exploded nearby had caused a suction that seemed to drag my very entrails downward and that pain was to stay with me for some considerable time.

The hospitality of the *Honeysuckle* crew was fantastic, cigarettes, tots, odd articles of clothing (in addition to survivors packs), mugs of steaming kye and the ever ready bucket kindly administered. We slept most of the time until we were transferred to the aircraft carrier HMS *Vindex* for treatment and passage home. Our debriefing and statements were taken aboard *Vindex* by our First Lieutenant Jimmy Dallaway and by the carrier's officers.

Nothing ever replaced the atmosphere of *Goodall*; even when I bought a forty-five foot sea cruiser and sailed her with my family and friends, *Goodall* was always uppermost in my mind. Who, other than another 'DE' man could even begin to understand? We were the last RN ship to be lost in the Battle of the Atlantic and the Arctic. Within a month of my arrival back in the UK I was on my way out to SEAC to serve on various craft.

Harry Carter, Telegraphist

I joined the ship as a telegraphist in Bangor, N.Ireland, soon after she came over from the States. My first trip was to Argentia (Newfoundland) and I was amazed at the facilities and amenities at the US Base there. Chatham Barracks would never be the same again! We did three trips to Iceland, two frigates escorting a large liner carrying reliefs for the troops there. We would be going flat out with the liner urging us to go faster. They really were rough trips and we would go in for repairs after each one. I only went ashore in Iceland once, which was not a pleasant experience as the natives were unfriendly and the prices high. A kroner was worth ninepence and an icecream cost three kroners, almost a day's pay.

We returned to Liverpool after escorting HMS *Nelson* to the D-Day landings and I went ashore to take an exam for Trained Operator. In my absence the ship refilled the oil tanks and they also filled the deck lockers on the messdeck which our kit was in. The Captain contacted (so he said) the Port Medical Officer who assured him there were no health risks in wearing the kit after it had been washed in the ship's laundry. Maybe not, but after washing, all the whites were now a lovely fawn colour which meant we had to replace them. The Captain had got himself off the hook at our expense and I never forgave him; to this day I consider we got a 'green rub'.

In August 1944 we escorted a convoy to Gibraltar and several incidents about that trip stand out in my mind. The first night in Gib the crew had shore leave and many came back to the ship the worse for wear, so the ship was in uproar until the early hours. Next morning the Captain cleared lower deck and issued a warning that if there was ever a repetition of the previous night's behaviour, leave would not be given again no matter where we were or how long we had been at sea. Next, we were hoisting the seaboat and when it reached the top it suddenly dropped, causing all who were manning the falls to go crashing into the depth-charge racks. How no one was injured I will never know. The third incident occurred at sea, when we challenged a ship and her reply was 'Pennant 01'. I looked up the pennant list and it wasn't allocated. I informed the bridge who challenged again and got the same reply so the Captain ordered our main armament (3 three-inch peashooters!) to be swung around and also illuminated the ship at the same time with our 24-inch searchlight. The ship turned out to be a cruiser, one of ours, thank God, HMS *Swiftsure*. As my coder remarked, she could have sunk us with a .303 rifle or hoisted us inboard!

The sinking of our 'chummy ship' HMS *Bullen* had a profound effect on our ship's crew and brought home to most of us how vulnerable we were. Little did we know that in just four months time we would find ourselves in the same situation.

On the night we were torpedoed I was standing in the W/T office flat talking to our P/O Tel. Looking out of the door leading to the superdeck we saw a U-boat blown to the surface and then sunk by gunfire. The Captain announced over the tannoy that we had a contact and were going in to attack it. The next thing I remember was the roar of flames and the sound of explosions, I thought we were being fired on. Looking up, all I could see were flames and looking across I saw the P/O Tel. slumped in the corner with his face blackened, then I passed out. The next thing I remember is lying at the edge of the deck looking into the water. I never saw or heard anyone around me; I was in a great deal of pain and had facial burns which prevented me from seeing clearly. I looked up and saw a ship coming through the mist and smoke. It touched briefly and hands reached over the rails and dragged me off. As the ship pulled away I was suspended by my arms which was most painful, as one of them had a compound fracture and the other one was burned and badly bruised from wrist to shoulder. I looked down and saw flames licking around my feet because the paintwork of the rescuing ship had caught alight. As I was pulled inboard I heard a voice say 'compound fracture', then I blacked out and some time later I found myself being strapped into a wraparound wooden stretcher and hearing a voice saying 'Christ, how much more of him is there?', due no doubt to the stretcher only reaching to my knees as I am well over six feet tall. Then I found myself in mid-air dangling from a crane and being transferred from ship to shore and put into an ambulance. As I was being taken into the hospital I looked up and saw a White Ensign over the doorway. I passed out again and the next thing I knew it was Tuesday. What happened to Monday I don't know.

After about four weeks in Vaenga Hospital I returned to Greenock in the sick bay of the aircraft carrier HMS *Queen* and spent the next six months in Mearnkirk Hospital near Glasgow.

The only other person to escape from the area where I was in the bridge structure wreckage was my friend and fellow telegraphist Doug Fenwick. He too managed to make his own way to the stern, but neither he nor I remember doing so. It was only in later years that I learned that no one could get up to where we were trapped because of the flames and exploding ammunition, also that the ship that rescued us was HMS *Honeysuckle*. Doug, who had a fractured skull and other injuries, was with me in Vaenga and Mearnskirk and we both left hospital at about the same time. I lost touch with him after that but traced him a couple of years ago and we had a reunion.

Having talked about our experiences and the research I had done, we came to the conclusion that I came to first and made my way to the stern. He later crawled out of the W/T Office onto the superdeck, was spotted by the crew at the stern and encouraged to make his way to them. We both agree we are two of the luckiest people alive. About three-quarters of the communications branch lost their lives. The ones I felt most keenly were my two very good friends, Sid Sivell Signalman (Trained Operator) my opposite number in the signals branch; and Telegraphist Bernard Cobb. We used to spend our leaves together in London as they were both Londoners. I used to stay at Bernard's parents house where his mother, a lovely lady, made me most welcome.

After many years searching I finally met the skipper of HMS *Honeysuckle* in 1992 at their annual reunion and was able to thank him for saving my life. I have since attended their reunions every year and have become firm friends with some of the crew, two of whom crewed the *Honeysuckle* seaboat which tragically overturned while picking up *Goodall* survivors from the sea. They were lucky to escape with their lives.

In conclusion, I would say I have good and bad memories of my time on *Goodall*. The food was grim and the living conditions left much to be desired. I made some good friends; the officers were rather remote, except our South African Gunnery Officer, who was very approachable and was always ready for a laugh with the lads.

Author's Note

Harry wrote to me after sending me the above:

Dear Vic,

Does your copy of the casualty list have the name of my namesake, another Carter who was a Stoker? He is not on the lists I have seen.

He went on to say, 'that Stoker Carter's parents received notice that he had been picked up and was in hospital, whereas my parents had received no notification at all. One of the survivors in hospital with me was a good friend of his and one day received a letter from Stoker Carter's parents asking if he knew which hospital he was in. Knowing that he had not survived the sinking he wrote back advising them to contact the Admiralty. I never did know the outcome but I know his name should be on the casualty list.'

Contacting the War Graves Commission website I found George Carter, Stoker 1st. Class RN died 29th April 1945 HMS Goodall. *His name is on the Chatham Memorial and can be found on the Roll of Honour in this book.*

Chief Motor Mechanic G Cook, C/MX 126486

I was at Action Stations in the after motor room when the explosion occurred. I was knocked out for about ten minutes. When I came round I saw that the port shaft had stopped and the tachometer was still showing 212 revolutions. One main engine was still running.

I tried to get the engine back on the board, but this was impossible and the lights had failed. I tried to get the emergency motor started but it stopped shortly afterwards. I then tried to get through by phone to Damage Control Headquarters and the forward motor control room, but this, too, was not possible. I then shut down the control board and closed the throttles. Then I went on deck with a view to getting forward but saw what had happened through the port hatch. Debris, fire and exploding ammunition prevented my going forward, so I went back to the motor room and told other ratings what had occurred and told them to make their way out and work aft. Then I, too, left as there was nothing further I could do.

Up to this time no water had entered my compartment and there was no fire. I could not close the escape hatch or the upper deck doors as they were damaged. I then made my way over the debris to the quarterdeck and helped the others under the direction of the First Lieutenant to ensure the after compartment water-tightness, and also helped clear away possible gear that would float and helped construct temporary rafts. I heard the First Lieutenant explain about the fire threat to the magazines as the fire was gaining aft. It appeared that the forward motor and engine room was well alight, and I was given the option of going over the side and make for the rafts, or else hold on to the stuff that had been thrown overboard, or to remain until the last possible moment. I then discovered that my lifebelt had been punctured so I decided to remain with the others and was eventually taken off by *Honeysuckle*.

George Halliday

I joined HMS *Goodall* in September 1944. She was part of the 19th Escort Group together with *Hesperus* (Senior Officer in command), *Bullen*, *Antigua*, *Anguilla* and *Loch Insh*. Our main function was to carry out anti-submarine sweeps in the North Atlantic, sometimes ahead of the convoy routes. This became a rather boring duty in that we would be at sea for 4/5 weeks with little to show for it. One day in port to refuel and re-victual and then off again for a similar stint, followed by seven days back in Liverpool, (not so boring!). Sometimes this routine was broken on receipt of a signal that aircraft had sighted a U-boat on the surface, when we would hare off at great speed to the reported position but no sign of the U-boat, if there had ever been one.

In December 1944 our luck changed with mixed results, and I was blooded into my first action. The location was just off Cape Wrath and after an all night sweep with *Goodall* taking the landward position, we were ordered by *Hesperus* to change places with *Bullen*. Shortly after, *Bullen* was torpedoed amidships and broke in two. We sent our whaler away to pick up survivors and were then ordered to carry out box searches with *Loch Insh*. In the mean time *Hesperus* took our position close to the stricken *Bullen*. Our whaler, which had picked up nine survivors, went alongside *Hesperus* to off-load, made fast with the painter, then without any warning *Hesperus* made off at great speed, capsizing the whaler and tragically adding to the casualties, which included three members of our whaler crew. We, with *Loch Insh* then made a contact and using the creeper tactic made several attacks. Eventually oil and debris came to the surface. We had made a kill, but because we had not stopped to pick up any of the debris, their Lordships at the Admiralty would only credit us with a possible.

I learnt many years later from the U-boat Archives that there had been two U-boats, U775 and U297. It was U775 that sank *Bullen* and U297 was sunk by *Goodall*. *Bullen* was a great loss; she had been laid down alongside *Goodall* in Boston and we had sailed together and come to regard her as our Chummy Ship. She was replaced by *Cotton* but it was never the same.

We went back to the old routine of A/S sweeps. In April we were ordered to join Convoy JW66 from the Clyde to Murmansk as one of the close escorts. This was something different and we sailed as a happy ship. The trip was quiet with a few skirmishes but no losses on either side and we anchored in Kola Bay waiting for the returning merchant ships. I did manage to get a run ashore but it was pretty dull. There was a narrow track which we were told not to wander from and to reinforce this about every 100 yards or so was an armed sentry, and any smiles or acknowledgement were met with a sullen stare; no eats or drinks and it was difficult to know one sex from the other!

April 29th saw what proved to be the last battle of the Arctic. We were ordered to sail in the new Convoy RA66 and we were informed that a large force of U-boats was waiting in the Kola Inlet. Information obtained subsequently from the U-boat archives named 14 boats and our orders were to clear the way for the convoy. We were joined by three other Escort Groups and very soon the sound of depth charges was heard. The first casualty was U-307, forced to the surface by a squid fired from *Loch Insh*. We were ordered to engage and this was my chance to fire my Oerlikon in anger for the first time. Whether I did any damage I will never know, but the tracers seemed to be on target.

U-307 was finally sunk by *Loch Insh's* main armament 4-inch shells. There were 14 survivors. *Goodall* then made a contact and was preparing to attack when she was struck by a torpedo fired by U-968. We were hit just forward of the bridge, igniting the 3-inch magazine and the explosion destroyed the forepart with the bridge with the mainmast being thrown back on the funnel. My action station was the Oerlikon on the starboard side just abaft the bridge, where the super deck buckled causing my gun mounting to collapse, trapping my right leg. Simultaneously I was struck on the head by falling debris. I was wearing sea boots and managed to wriggle my leg free and with a tingling feeling in my face. and blood running from my head I was able to lower myself on to the main deck and make my way aft. There were about 40 members of the crew with the First Lieutenant on the quarterdeck. The fire was intense, spreading from the bridge and enveloping the waist. Ammunition was exploding, but there was no power to enable us to fight the fire which was now spreading rapidly aft. The First Lieutenant gave the order to abandon ship. I went over the side and clambered on to a Carley raft which soon became heavily laden with about 14 either in it or clinging on to the sides.

We were ordered to pull away, which gave us the opportunity to see the damage to *Goodall*. From what would normally be the break on a destroyer nothing forward remained. Approximately 30 minutes later a surface ship, I think it was *Farnham Castle*, approached to pick us up, but as she closed in we saw the attack pennant unfurling. She had made a contact, and went past us at speed, her bow wave causing the raft to capsize, throwing us into the sea, I came to the surface and saw the raft about 100 yards away and swam to it. There were only four of us who made it; the rest perished. We then saw that the sea was on fire from the escaping diesel and with no means of propulsion we were being slowly overtaken by the flames. It was pretty scary.

We were finally picked up by a Russian Motor Torpedo Boat. They treated us very well, stripping us of our sodden oily clothes and using old rags they bathed us from a bucket of vodka. I assume this was for some anti-frost reason. I was then given a mug of vodka to drink and they took us to the RNAH at Vaenga. I must have passed out as I have no memory of the next three hours or so; possibly the vodka was the reason. I regained consciousness as I was being taken on board *Vindex* as a cot case direct to the sickbay where my wounds were treated. Back in the UK I was transferred to the hospital ship *Isle of Jersey* en route to Kingseat Hospital, Aberdeen, and diagnosed with first degree burns of the face, third degree burns on the right leg and lacerations of the scalp.

Going back to the action at the Kola Inlet a second U-boat, U-286 was sunk by *Anguilla* and *Cotton*.

On a lighter note, we all have our memories some good some not so good. The strange thing is that while the traumas remain, it is the less serious memories that stand out. I had been knocked about a bit and returned to the UK on *Vindex*. There, I was placed in a small ward next to the bulkhead door alongside a wash basin. Not feeling too good, and with bandages must have looked like the invisible man, I had no idea who the other patients were, as a curtain was drawn across the length of the ward. With no portholes and dimmed lights it was quite eerie.

Suddenly, there was an almighty kerfuffle with lots of loud expletives, it was real lower deck language, and only what can be described as an apparition dashed past the foot of my bed. Dressed in a white operating smock, still cussing it made straight for the wash basin. Hoisting up his smock and dumping his family jewels in the basin and turned the cold water tap on. I thought what the hell was all this about, after a short time he disappeared behind the curtain still swearing.

The following morning I found out the reason behind this strange behaviour. There were six other patients in the ward, all circumcision cases who had had the snip earlier in. the day, and it would appear that matey had been sat up in bed reading a book, when he came across a very very erotic chapter, with painful results. Needless to say the trip to the wash basin was to dampen his ardour.

Well, it cheered ME up!.

Following an invitation from the crew of U-968 to join them at their reunion in Germany, and after canvassing other survivors of *Goodall*, George Halliday and Cyril Lovitt attended the reunion from 23rd to26th May 2002 at Plau am See. George Halliday reported:

Arriving at Hamburg we travelled to Laboe to visit the U-boat Memorial and go aboard the beached U-995. it was a strange feeling to see the inside of one of our old adversaries, we also visited the Kiel

Canal, Rostock and Warnemunde, then on to Plau am See for the reunion with excursions to Scherwin and Lubz which is the home of my U-boat correspondent Gerhard Bigalke, where two rooms in his house have been set aside and dedicated to models, photographs and artifacts of U-968 and *Goodall* giving details of the of the 29th April 1945 battle. The reunion itself was quite informal with speeches of welcome which were suitably responded to; there was very lIttle talk of the war, the impression was that they wanted to forget it

We then moved on to Osterode am See and for the next four days visited sites in the Harz Mountains including Duderstart, a well known beauty spot. On a more sombre note was the visit to the Grenzland Museum at the old border between East and West Germany. It was quite eerie standing in the original watch tower where East German guards had kept watch and were ever ready to shoot fellow East Germans trying to cross to the west.

There is still a marked difference between East and West Germany and it will take at least another ten years to bring about real reunification. Remember the old GDR existed for over 45 years.

Cyril and I agreed that we were both glad that we accepted the invitation and that the genuine friendship and hospitality was something special.

There are still 29 of the boat's crew alive, most of whom were in attendance. Their Captain, Oberleutnant Otto Westphalen was present as were most of the officers.

Author's Note

Time and time again over the years the question has cropped up among the group of known survivors as to how many in total survived the carnage and there has never been a satisfactory answer. Efforts made at navy reunions to locate any others outside of the known group have met with only limited success. The ship's complement figures vary from different sources and the true numbers when she left UK on this, her last voyage, have yet to be discovered. Both George and myself have made many enquiries on this question which is still ongoing, with George carrying out further research.

Temporary Lieutenant (E) William H Henderson RNR
Engineer Officer

The ship had been at Action Stations from 1655, I being at Damage Control Headquarters. At approximately 1930 the order 'Stand By Hedgehog' was given and a few minutes later an explosion occurred. After recovering from the shock, during which time debris was falling around, I took a quick survey. The forward part of the ship had disappeared and the bridge was lying over what remained of the funnel and overhanging the starboard side.

The ship's normal power had failed and attempts were made to start the emergency generator, which was unsuccessful. By this time a fire athwartships had a good hold and the Oerlikon magazine was going off in all directions. With no electric power, the only other fighting equipment onboard were the petrol driven billies, only one of which could be found on the quarter deck and which was damaged by debris.

The forward engine room was damaged and filled with smoke, but due to the conditions I was unable to make an examination. All other compartments of the forward engine room were watertight up to the main deck but the watertight doors and hatches were distorted. With no firefighting equipment to tackle the fire which was nearing the 3-inch magazine the, First Lieutenant ordered the crew, who were by this time mustered on the quarterdeck, to cut adrift the Carley floats and take to the water. A few ratings preferred to stay behind with the First Lieutenant and myself and improvised floats were made. A few casualties which we were able to find were brought to the quarterdeck. Soon afterwards HMS *Honeysuckle* came alongside and the few casualties and the remainder of the crew were taken onboard.

Fred W. James

I left Scotland aboard *Queen Elizabeth* to New York, where we berthed next to the French liner *Normandie*. It had been sabotaged and was listing about 49 degrees. After New York we went to Asbrey Park New Jersey and after staying there for a few weeks or more we came back to Boston, Charleston dockyard. On the 11th October 1943 we commissioned *Goodall*, and from there we went to Bermuda 'working up' with *Aylmer* and *Bentley*, returning to Boston with engine trouble. After leaving Boston with *Aylmer* and *Bentley* we joined the convoy back to U.K.

On the 5th June 1944 we escorted the battleship HMS *Nelson* with HMSs. *Duncan* and *Bullen* to Cherbourg. Then we were called away

30

to Gladstone Dock, Liverpool.

On 18th November 1944 we were sweeping in the Cape Wrath area and that was where HMS *Bullen* was torpedoed. We came back to Gladstone Dock where we were given new clothing and we knew we were going somewhere cold. Our guess was right - Russia! We were part of 19th Escort Group and were sent ahead of the returning convoy RA66 to clear the way through the U-Boat pack waiting for us. As we were sweeping the Kola inlet one of the U-boats came to the surface damaged and the crew were coming out of the conning tower while we were shelling it. Next thing I knew I was in the water. I never even heard the explosion, all I remember is debris falling down on me. I'm not a good swimmer but I managed to hold onto a Carley raft with about ten others also hanging onto it. The raft turned over a few times and with all the sea alight HMS *Honeysuckle* went between the raft and the burning sea. The most frightening thing was they were dropping depth charges round us. In the meantime I took all my clothing off to keep afloat and after a while I was picked up by a Russian Torpedo boat which took us to Murmansk. I was still there on VE Day. Later I was sent back home in HMS *Cassandra*.

Steve Keeler (Survivor of HMS Bullen). Memories of HMS Goodall.

My memories of her are a bit vague after all these years. We sailed together protecting wartime convoys to and fro across the North Atlantic. There was always a bit of competition between us, but in a very friendly way. Alongside the jetty, be it Liverpool or Belfast there was always a standing joke over whose ship's side was the cleanest. Crossing each other's gang-plank for a run ashore or just to empty the gash there was always the usual friendly banter but ashore or afloat we were two of a kind, both dedicated to hunting down the enemy and protecting the convoy in our care. If we saw each other in trouble ashore the cry went up, 'EG19' and we were always there to help each other. *Goodall* was the first to our aid at our torpedoing on Dec.6th 1944 and although in different parts of the world when we heard of her loss, the toast at the bar or at 'tot' time was 'HMS *Goodall*.'

PO (LTO) Robert V R Knighton C/SSX 23691

At the time of the explosion I was on the quarterdeck in charge of depth-charge crews, when out of the corner of my eye I saw a large yellow and red flash and debris started falling immediately afterwards, so I dived for cover under the depth charge rails. When all the debris had finished flying I immediately thought of the depth charges, and checked that all were set to safe and disconnected the primer safety gear. I then reported to the First Lieutenant that all depth charges were to SAFE. I then gave a hand to get the injured together and helped clear away Carley floats over the side. There was not much we could do after this. The fire amidships was well alight, and when the First Lieutenant ordered us to abandon ship I jumped into the floatnet expecting others to follow my lead.

We drifted around and the burning oil was very close and we were practically into it when HMS *Honeysuckle* rescued us. We had six men on the floatnet of whom we lost one, Stoker Worthy.

Cyril Arnold Lovitt, Second Lieutenant, HMS Goodall

I was Temporary Lieutenant RNVR and joined *Goodall* when she was refitted at Belfast in January 1944. My previous ship was one of the old Town Class, HMS *Ripley*, one of the 50 WW1 US destroyers that the Yanks gave us under Lend Lease. We had delivered her to the Russians at South Shields.

When *Goodall* was sunk I was at my action station on the bridge as gunnery control officer. I stood on a wooden structure and crouching underneath working, would you believe, a Battenberg course and speed indicator, invented during the first World War. There were two ratings, one of whom was John Goss. I am pretty sure that he and I were the only two to survive from the bridge.

Sub-Lieutenant Geoffrey Hadden, who was a good chum of mine, was in the plot. He was the pilot and was picked up by the Russians. I was told later that we were the only convoy to receive any help from the Russians.

I can well recall standing, well propped up really, because my pelvis had been fractured and my right leg was inoperable, by the depth charge rails in the stern. The Chief was with me and we were looking forward at what appeared to be a large jagged piece of deck pointing to the sky. I said something like 'Christ, Chief is that us' and he said 'Yes, laddie it is' The torpedo had hit us square on the bow and blown us wide open as far as the back of the bridge. I was fortunate in that I was thrown back from the bridge and was found in the Y gun turret. The No 1, Jimmy Dallaway, had given instructions that all dead bodies should be ditched, so I must have shown signs of life. I remember the corvette that nudged into our stern enabling me to be hauled across without getting my feet wet. The next thing I remember was sitting up below decks propped up against the bulkhead complaining bitterly that I had lost my new cap and No 1 refused my request to be taken off to return home in *Vindex*.

Author's Note

This was an e-mail sent to me from Australia in response to a plea I put out on the internet for Goodall *survivors. This was followed by Cyril's story.*

HMS GOODALL*: My Story*

I joined *Goodall* in Belfast where she had arrived from the USA in January 1944. She was undergoing a minor refit designed to bring her more into line with British standards; in other words, to civilize her and get rid of the American excesses such as no scuttles in the cabins, steel decking painted brick red with some fireproof substance. I gathered that on the way over Jimmy (First Lieutenant) disposed of much of the steel wardroom furniture, 'lost at sea', though how the wardroom table and chairs made it to the upper deck was not explained. Good cork lino was laid, wooden table and upholstered seats installed and scuttles cut in the ship's side. We never did get rid of the cabin curtains of spun glass or whatever, fireproof. The Yanks seemed to have a thing about fire proofing.

The stories the lads told about their experiences in the States when they picked up the ship filled me with envy. It seems, if they are to be only half believed, they were literally accosted by nubile young women ready to jump into bed any time anywhere.

Shortly after we left Belfast we went to Gladstone Dock in Bootle which was to become our 'home'. It was not long before we sailed to take up escort duty with an Atlantic convoy. I remember our station was on the starboard side of the convoy doing no more than 8 knots. I was very sick but I had been warned to make sure that there was something inside me and so I carried dry toast in my pocket and lived for the ten or so days that it took to reach Argentia, Newfoundland, on dry toast and duffle coat fluff. We had a metal wastepaper basket on the bridge so that we didn't make too much mess. On that convoy we saw at least two ships sunk on the port side I remember seeing the brilliant orange red flash in the sky. We must have been detached from the main convoy as we approached port because I remember seeing ice floes around the ship as we made for Newfoundland.

It was our first taste of American navy ways and we were enormously impressed with being able to walk to a shore telephone and call for 'Transportation' to take us to the Officers Club. Argentia was one of the bases that Churchill swapped for the fifty clapped out

Town Class destroyers that the Americans gave us .One of them, *Ripley*, was my first ship. Jimmy was also impressed because he was able to get the Yanks to spray paint the upper works. It took them one morning if I remember correctly.

I suppose we must have returned with another convoy but I have no clear recollection of it except that at some stage we were ordered to sink what remained of the bows of a ship that had been torpedoed. I remember that our so called 'armour- piercing' shells bounced off the hull like pebbles skimming through water.

Having diesel-electric propulsion we were not popular at any base if we needed maintenance. It was not unusual for us to be headed for, say, Liverpool and be told to go to Gourock. Chief would spend long hours poring over ship's drawings trying to work out how to get some vital piece of machinery out and sent ashore.

Being ship's Correspondence Officer in addition to Sports Officer and Divisional Officer for the Forecastle Division, I had my hands full. As soon as we did make it to Gladstone Dock I would get the money for the ship's pay and then drive out to some posh suburb to collect the new CB's (code books) and all the amendments thereto. A job I did in my spare time! Oh yes Jimmy wanted to use the sports equipment that had been issued to the ship in America, so I collected Sports Officer and Education Officer. I remember the horrified reaction that Jimmy had when he saw the shorts that were part of the sports gear. The inside leg measurement was about one inch and he wouldn't allow anyone to have them. I doubt that the men would have touched them anyway.

We did a couple of runs to Iceland with a trooper and that was the most uncomfortable sea I ever remember; it was pitch and toss all the way and at fourteen knots we had to zig-zag at about eighteen to provide any sort of screen. It was at Reykjavik my command of the anchor was exposed for the sham it was. The harbour is beautifully clear and very deep. When given the order to slip, the anchor with its cable following roared out at lightning speed in a cloud of rusty dust. I hadn't a clue how much had gone and neither had anyone else, certainly not my party of brave hearties standing around looking shocked and not a little amused. Not so James Dallaway, who put on one of his displays of violent anger and abuse directed at the entire forecastle in general and me in particular!

We became part of a support group aimed at strengthening the escort as the convoys left Western Approaches and again as they returned.

Attack from the air was a constant worry and we had to try to improve our aircraft recognition with the aid of little plastic model aeroplanes, quite neat little things really. One would first look at the name printed underneath and then brandish the thing at the lookout and challenge him to identify it. 'Junkers 88' was a fairly common response. The rule of thumb was, if he gets too close, let him have it, but we did always recognise the stringbag.

A trip to Gib provided a pleasant break and the Skipper, Lt-Cdr J.V. Fulton (peace time RNVR) assembled a supply of empty rum jars which were duly filled with the very cheap but excellent Spanish sherry. Several of the lads got horribly sunburnt on that trip. When we were in Gib I went ashore with Mick Armstrong and Geoffrey Hadden, two other subs, and we were taken in tow by a helpful Spaniard who seemed to be an itinerant barber. He showed us the bullring and pointed out the spot in the sand that was stained red with the blood of the bulls who all seemed to have been killed more or less in the one place.

We quaffed a fair measure of sherry, all, it seemed, at one peseta or roughly sixpence a glass. Our friend then decided or probably Mick suggested that we should visit a brothel. It was a total fiasco because although the available talent was duly paraded for our inspection and at one stage came and sat on our laps. Mine was a particularly plump, sweaty lady. We found that our total resources were not enough for even one lady and we lacked the guts anyway!

Back at Gladstone Dock we found that the Bird Class sloops were in port. They were commanded by a famous Captain whose name escapes me and had the reputation for sinking a number of U-boats especially in the Bay of Biscay. They had perfected the square search and, finding an asdic contact, would set up a box round the spot with one ship traversing inside the square. They would drop a creeping depth-charge pattern at 8 knots and succeed in springing the plates round the stern (their own, that is). We saw them come in with a noticeable list and leave the same way. *Black Swan* and *Magpie* were two I remember. We envied them their two twin Bofors mountings just abaft the bridge.

Talking of guns, I had by now become the so-called Gunnery Control Officer and a sort of wooden bandstand was built at the back of the bridge and this was my station from where, in theory, I 'controlled' the four 3-inch and 22 Oerlikons. We also had hedgehog, four throwers and two rails. It seemed that every time we put in for maintenance they would find a space to put another Oerlikon. AB

John Goss and another whose name I forget actually sat under my band stand and operated a Battenberg Course and Speed Indicator but since this was designed for surface action and our armament was so light it is difficult to imagine the circumstances in which we would ever have used this antique piece of equipment.

In June 1944, the day after D-day, we escorted *Nelson* into the Channel from Pompey while she did her coastal bombardment. On the way back, it was a bright sunny day and our peace was rudely interrupted by one of the lookouts reporting gunfire on the starboard quarter and we actually came under fire from the shore battery on Jersey or Guernsey. Later we seemed to find ourselves sent to look for subs that were believed to be snorkelling round coastal waters near Marazion.

Then we must have made our way North because I distinctly remember the morning that our chummy ship *Bullen* was torpedoed off the North coast of Scotland. I remember it seemed quite unreal to watch her slowly break in half and sink. An exercise with a Polish sub was conducted near Lough Foyle and I was privileged to go aboard and go on a trip as she listened for the escorts clattering overhead. Mills bombs were dropped to simulate depth charges. It was alarming to realise just how vulnerable we were to their hydrophones. I nearly came to a sticky end on this trip. We were to practice boarding a surfaced boat, the object being to get down below locate the CBs (Confidential Books) and prevent the crew from scuttling. I was put in charge of the boarding party, armed with a thunderflash, a bakelite mills bomb with a detonator connected to a ring on the end of a tape that went round one's finger, a revolver and a length of rope and a canvas bag.

The procedure was to pull alongside, leap onto the sub's deck trying not to slip arse over tip on the slippery surface, run to the conning tower, yell 'Under below', fling down the thunderflash to intimidate the enemy, slide down the internal ladder, chalk an arrow on the deck to indicate the bow and rush to the Captain's cabin and seize the CBs. Oh yes, I had a hand axe to break into the cupboard where the CBs were conveniently kept, we hoped. In the meantime my trusty men were dealing with the demoralised crew and shutting the stopcocks.

It so happens that on this particular boat was a young Pole who had only very recently escaped from Poland, spoke no English and when he heard the commotion ran to the bottom of the ladder I was descending and was waiting for me with a knife. He was convinced they were being taken by Germans. Fortunately for me an officer saw the glint of the knife blade and prevented a nasty accident!

I omitted to mention that I was also the cypher officer and coming off watch I would invariably be required to decypher messages that the sparks had picked up giving details of the latest action in the channel, in the Atlantic or anywhere else that the Old Man was interested in. They were of no conceivable use to us but he liked to be kept informed.

It was around this time, I suppose, that Knocker Whyte, our Second Lieutenant, got a posting and the Skipper on one occasion when I was taking him some cypher messages asked me if it was not time that I was promoted Lieutenant. I had been a sub since I joined in 1942.

So I became Second Lieutenant and the Skipper got his wish to be sent on a Russian convoy; and Knocker Whyte actually volunteered to come with us and got his posting delayed.

CONVOY JW/RA 66

Now, as the words of that extremely rude song would have it, we come to the vital bit. I suspect, although I have no way of ever proving it, our somewhat strange skipper J.V.Fulton, Lt-Cdr RNVR (peacetime, or have I mentioned that before), son of a wealthy family of shipbuilders on the Clyde, had a hankering to go on a Russian Convoy and finally got his wish. The only other person on board who seemed to welcome this prospect, so far as I can recall, was Knocker Whyte. He, too, was peacetime RNVR and came from a wealthy family of industrialists in Darlington. He had served in full-rigged sailing ships as part of his education and had served in a trawler called *Lord Austin*. They had been part of the escort for a previous Russian convoy and when they arrived in Murmansk they were sent with one or two ships round to Archangel.When they finally returned to the Kola Inlet their return convoy had sailed leaving them stranded. Came the next arrival and, you've guessed, because they 'knew the way' they were sent off to Archangel again with a couple of merchantmen. This went on it seems for a very long time. They ran out of stores and had to beg and borrow to keep going. Now there's a story for you, the forgotten men! Anyhow, when Knocker heard that we were off to Russia although he had received his posting he volunteered to sail with the *Goodall* and Fulton arranged it. We must have sailed from Gladstone Dock and joined the convoy somewhere in Northern waters. We were in support sailing ahead of the convoy together with a group of corvettes.

The passage north was uneventful. I remember the big 'O' Class minelaying destroyers laying mines as we reached the inlet. We had a go at a submarine with depth charges I think and we gathered up some evidence but I don't recall that we were ever credited with a kill. It was not uncommon, as you no doubt know, for U-boats to shoot bits of debris out of the tubes to give the impression of having been hit. Even what looked like human remains were suspect because they would use pig remains which of course resemble human parts.

Once alongside we were allowed ashore and I remember it seemed to be a Godforsaken place. There was still snow on the ground and I remember feeling sorry for a lone sentry standing under a sort of umbrella shelter in the middle of a road intersection. We wandered into a cinema which was free and saw a film of Sonja Henje skating. The houses were drab grey wooden buildings apparently without any paint and hardly a single soul to be seen anywhere.

At one point during our stay Jimmy announced that there would be a whaler race and we were duly conscripted to sail our whaler in competition with those from some of the other escorts. It was a beautiful clear sunny day and we rounded the stern of *Royal Sovereign* (known as The Tiddly Quid) which was one of the ships we had given the Russians. I don't think she ever left the anchorage but she was beautifully painted.

Moving along to the day of departure, 29 April it was as I remember, a clear calm day and we sailed ahead of the convoy astern of the group of corvettes. One of the corvettes attacked a U-boat and forced her to the surface. There was fair chaos as we all banged away at the surfaced sub whose crew very bravely manned their gun and actually got one round away. It seems only minutes later that our asdic reported an echo fine on the starboard bow. I am fairly certain I heard the echo over the speaker. There was a fair amount of modified panic on the bridge, I think I ordered all guns bearing Green 05. Jimmy was, I think, there but quickly resumed his action station on the quarterdeck. The order to step aside was never given and the next thing I remember was a vivid orange flash and then nothing until I found myself propped up right aft between the two sets of rails looking for'ard. Chief was there and as I think I said previously I could see the jagged edge of decking sticking up before the mast. I do remember the ship that nudged her bows into our stern and I was presumably hauled across the gap. I came to below decks and was propped up against the bulkhead, At this stage the shortening in my right leg, I was later told, was about four inches. Jimmy was talking to us, I seem to remember that there were quite a few of us semi-walking wounded although I don't think any of us could have actually walked. Some of the lads were told that they would go back in the carrier. We were carried by stretcher to the small RN Auxiliary Hospital so called which seemed to be the upper storey of a sort of warehouse. I must have been put into a large plaster cast which stretched from my waist to my ankles because my next recollection is of having this contraption removed while I was fully conscious and it hurting like hell. There was someone armed with what seemed to be a very large pair of loppers cutting away at the plaster. I asked for a shot of something and they gave me one.

I don't remember much for the next few days except a SBA trying hard to take an X-ray with a Mickey Mouse machine that apparently could not penetrate my pelvis. Came VE Day and I was offered a tumbler of neat rum to celebrate, which I declined. I had no great liking for rum because when as Officer of the Day on board I had to supervise the rum issue this entailed going down below decks right forward through the paint locker to get to the rum store. The stink of the paint combined with the strong aroma of the neat rum was almost too much for my vulnerable stomach. The lads knew this of course and my supervision was at best cursory.

In the bed next to me was Johnny Goss who was in a very bad way. Not only was his right leg shattered but a rope had been tied round him before he was thrown overboard and this had burned the skin under his chin from the chest up. I remember he moaned quite a bit and some of the lads were not too sympathetic. I remember the McKillop brothers, one of whom had a badly fractured arm and the blood seemed to be seeping through the plaster. They seemed to have got themselves a sort of working party job shifting stores and this enabled them to borrow sufficient of the stores which when sold to the Russians raised enough money to enable us to send telegrams to our families.

Being the only officer present I was entrusted with the loot and I am ashamed to say that I still have a few Russian bank notes among my souvenirs, also a very crude knife made from perspex and metal salvaged from a crashed aircraft. I must have been presented with this by one of the lads.

We were all brought back on the last convoy aboard a carrier. They had me in a small cabin all on my own at first but the arrangement didn't suit me because I wanted to be with the lads and I had I suppose a certain feeling of responsibility for Johnny Goss who was in my division. My leg by this time was in a Thomas Splint which was designed to stretch it to something like its normal length. I remember the panic when an aircraft was catapulted off the ship and we imagined that we had been hit. There was a half-hearted attempt to get us out fortunately stopped by one of the crew who clearly thought we were mad.

Arriving back in the Clyde we were taken to the Naval Hospital at Mearnskirk just outside Glasgow. There normal naval custom prevailed and we were separated but the lads did come to see me and I remember a charming gentle physio with ginger hair who managed to get some life back into my leg, pleading with me to make a 'macrame' belt 'for my girl friend' in order to stimulate the lads, who had firmly resisted any idea of therapy, into proving that they could do better. I am afraid I rather lost touch after that. I was discharged in about September and finally demobbed in September 1946 after finishing as a Personnel Selection Officer at *Royal Arthur*, Corsham.

Johnny Goss did call on me once at our home in Barnet. He was in a wheel chair but had been taken back to a job with Hoover the vacuum cleaner people, I wonder whether he survived.

And that is my story, that is my song, we've been in the Andrew too bloody long, so roll on the Rodney, the Nelson, Renown. We can't say the Hood 'cos the bastard's gone down.

There was the chief engineer from Perth, RNR, but his name escapes me. Our first Gunner was a South African, P D Mallet, a splendid dedicated man.

Author's Note

The famous Captain referred to was Captain Johnnie Walker RN and his ship HMS Starling, Pennant No U66.

Johnny Goss survived for some years after the war despite his disabilities. Sadly he 'crossed the bar' a few years ago.

The carrier referred to was HMS Queen, a RN Escort Carrier. Cyril was brought back in the sick bay with several others.

Sub-Lt Paul Mallett
Author's Note
Sub-Lt Paul Mallett was Gunnery Officer on Goodall from the beginning of her commission until January 1945 when he was drafted off. To use his own words, he was sad to leave his special ship.

I can understand his feelings because when in contact with members of the ship's company I find they had high regard for him and even now he keeps in touch with those who are left. He was the only South African on Goodall and he wrote of early days on the ship and of D-Day 1944. I quote the following from his notes:

Paul Mallett firmly believed his draft off the ship at Liverpool probably saved his life and when asked about the war would reply, 'We didn't hate the Germans; we would try to kill them of course but if we blew their U-boats to the surface we would give them succour. You forgive, but you can't forget and you always remember those who fell in the war.'

He is still enjoying life in his native South Africa and still in contact wit ex-shipmates.

He supplied the Goodall log giving brief details of her movements.

It was early morning on D-Day and with our sister ship HMS *Bullen* and the destroyer HMS *Duncan* we escorted HMS *Nelson* to ten miles off the coast of Cherbourg. She was one of the capital ships to bombard the German positions on the Normandy coast. The Admiral in *Nelson* asked 'Would you like to stay and watch the fireworks?' We were unable to as we had other demands on our time, to act as a fast escort of a transport to Iceland before we returned to the English Channel to support the operation there.

Chief ERA Charles R. Martin C/M 38753
I was in the forward motor room at the time, the speed of the ship being 212 revolutions (8 knots). Propulsion stopped dead on both shafts as soon as the ship was struck and lights failed then came back on momentarily. All auxiliary machinery had stopped.

We left the motor room and saw the fire on the upper deck and tried the fire-plugs, but saw no water was coming. The generator was still running in the after engine room and I was just going down when it stopped. I then searched for auxiliary fire-fighting appliances but all were either damaged or missing from stowage. As nothing more could be done I started with others carrying out the First Lieutenant's orders to get water tightness in the after part of the ship. After we had done all we could in this direction we went on the gun deck to see if any casualties were around and assisted them to the quarterdeck.

We assembled aft and the First Lieutenant explained the fire danger to the magazine and gave us the option to either jump clear and swim after the rafts or stay until the last possible moment for which we started to make temporary rafts from spars and timber. I also helped to put on rope tails for lashing the men to spars. We were eventually taken off by HMS *Honeysuckle* which proceeded to rescue men from Carley rafts and floatnets. I assisted men from the floatnets inboard and I consider that all that could possibly be done on HMS *Goodall* was done and there was no panic. Everyone carried out orders as required.

ERA George Mason C-MX 116397

I was in the forward motor room at action stations. Speed of the ship was 212 revolutions at the time of the explosion. Right away I realised that we had been hit forward and the ship took a list to starboard. I immediately closed the throttles and number two engine was still running. Then I broke the switches on the switchboard and saw the fire-flushing pump was stopped due to the switch tripping. Also I remember seeing the motor panel come partly adrift and some switches were partly made. I then switched off number two boiler and came up the hatch to the starboard side and closed the upper deck hatch, then tried to close the upper deck door but was unable to do so. Then I crossed over to the port side during which time I could hear the engines running in the after engine room. I saw the Chief ERA and the First Lieutenant; they wanted hoses rigged to control the fires on the upper deck. Making my way to the forward motor room with the intention of trying to start the fire and flushing pump I noticed as I reached the motor room hatch that the lights were on in the room, then they flickered for a short while, then went out. I realised that the power had failed and it was useless to try to start the pump and I remember standing alongside the Chief ERA while he tried the fire main on deck, but there was no pressure. I then went aft to the port side by crawling under the debris and I reached the quarterdeck and helped to assist hands to clear away the floatnet, then proceeded to number four Carley float forward, but wreckage of mast and bridge was too bad for it to be cleared. I then obeyed the First Lieutenant's order to get into the Carley floats with the Chief Stoker and other hands. There were about eighteen to twenty in the float. When away from the ship I saw the flames all around the bridge and the wireless office. At the same time Oerlikon magazines were exploding and oil from the forward fuel tanks burning and spreading on the water. We capsized three times, losing a seaman the first time and Stoker Carter the second; and the last time we lost Stoker Harling. After about three-quarters of an hour we were picked up by a whaler and as we were going alongside HMS *Farnham Castle* the whaler capsized and left only six of those originally on the Carley float.

Freddie Peeters

I joined HMS *Goodall* 8th September 1944. The day she was torpedoed I had just left the wheelhouse on the way to my 'action station' on the depth-charges when there was an almighty explosion and I was thrown to the deck. I got up, rather dazed and noted that half the ship was missing, ammunition was exploding all around me and as I crawled aft I could see limbs lying around. It was terrible, a duffle coat lay near with just an arm in the sleeve. Reaching the port side I jumped into the icy water and got onto a raft with six others. The sea to starboard was well alight, caused by calcium flares which had ignited the fuel from our tanks ripped open by the explosion. It was HMS *Farnham Castle*, I believe, which put scramble nets out for us to grab but got a 'ping' from her ASDIC and picking up speed tipped our Carley raft over and once again we were up to our necks in the very cold water. There were only four of us left then and luckily we were picked up by a Russian MTB. I tried to move but couldn't because my left leg had no feeling in it by then and after about another five minutes I think I would have given up and joined the other shipmates that had been lost. One of the Russian sailors picked me up like a piece of frozen meat then I was stripped off, rubbed down with vodka and given some of it to drink, then laid across the diesel engine casing. Coming to at the Kola Inlet, we were well looked after. I also remember that while in the sea I could feel the shock waves from exploding depth-charges and rolling myself into a ball to protect my stomach.

We were brought back to Scapa on *Vindex* and were the last of the warships to be sunk in the war in Europe.

Author's Notes

Fate dealt a cruel blow to some: Leading Signalman John (Eddie) Rawlinson joined Goodall *in Liverpool at the beginning of her last and fatal voyage. He was one of several replacements of the ship's company who were drafted off the ship for various reasons, promotion, courses, end of time or compassionate grounds etc.*

Tragically he was lost on the day the ship was sunk. There is every possibility that his action station could have been on or near the bridge along with the Captain, Gunnery Officer and others who did not survive or were badly injured when the torpedo struck. His name is on the list of those missing, believed killed, and was never found. It is particularly sad as he had served throughout the war and had survived to the point when the war was almost over, so there would have been every possibility of his chance for an early demob.

His son Michael contacted me in response to a plea on the internet and along with his mother had been looking for the true facts for the past fifty years or more and they have gathered much information over those years. They have found it to be a moving experience having contact with several of the Goodall survivors and during visits to dedication services and matters to do with the Arctic campaign.

Michael said 'My parents were married in January 1945 during a home leave and after only a few weeks of marriage my father sailed on that last Russian convoy of WW2. I was born in October 1945 so never knew my father, although my mother tells me that he knew I was on the way.

After Goodall was sunk, the circumstances in which my mother received the terrible news was even more distressing than would have been expected, due to the fact that my parents had only been married for a matter of weeks while my father was on leave. The change of 'next of kin' details had not reached the relevant department; consequently a telegram was sent to Eddie's father in Brighton informing him of the loss. He assumed that my mother had also been told and unfortunately wrote to her in London and that is how she learnt the loss of my father.'

As fate dealt a cruel blow to some it looked kindly on others.
Ivan Chappell was one of those drafted off the ship at Liverpool to go on a course for his higher rate, I believe. He had already cheated death on at least one occasion, on December 6th when Bullen, their 'chummy' sister ship was torpedoed.

Goodall launched their seaboat at that time to pick up survivors, with Ivan Chappell as the coxswain. The seaboat full of survivors was capsized and an unknown number were lost. Three of the seaboat's crew were among them but Ivan luckily was picked up some time later. The other two of the crew were never found. Their names have been added to the roll of honour in this book.

A/B G.A. Roy, C/JX 678164

Recalling the events that led up to the loss of HMS *Goodall* (K479) as I saw them, it happened so long ago that I'm afraid some of the finer points such as times and dates may be awry; however I'll give it my best shot.

On the 29th April 1945 we, in company with others of the 19th Escort Group, set sail down the Kola Inlet towards the Barents Sea. The scene was pretty tranquil, my feelings were, like most of my oppos, let's get the hell out of here and get back to Blighty, Bootle Docks, Lime Street and crumpet! There was a buzz going around the ship that there were U-Boats on the prowl outside the Inlet, but one had the comfort in the knowledge we as a tried and tested group could give the subs a bloody nose. We had a meal around the usual time 1700 hrs.or thereabouts, the ship then alerted to anti-sub stations i.e, Hedgehog and Depth-charge crews closed up, I can't say when we went to full action stations however I think it was around the first contact by the group on subs.

My station being No.1 on the Oerlikon above the W/T caboosh just aft of the funnel deck, port side. My No.2 was Norman Keyes who had come through with me in the same class.

We noticed a bit of high jinks with *Loch Insh* out to starboard, then a U-Boat bow shot to the surface, all hell broke loose with 20mm. shells hitting the hull and conning tower. We could see the poor buggers diving overboard or being shot to pieces. Not a pretty sight. I believe 14 survived from U-307.

No sooner had the furore subsided when I heard the yardarm pulleys working. I looked up and I saw the black flag flying. I remember thinking Christ! another 'Ping' (contact). They must be thick around here. I remember clearly feeling uneasy as if a premonition, something was going to happen, it was uncanny. Picture the scene, secured to my gun by a hefty leather belt, gun ready with french letter off the end of the barrel (saves water going up the spout), my mate with ammo locker ready, the same scenario with other gun crews on the funnel deck.

Then at 1930 approx (I was told later), there was a terrific flash followed by flying debris, something big slammed into my gun shield knocking the magazine flying off the gun and twisted the right hand side of the armour-plate shield. I'm certain that shield saved my life then. I was left hanging by the straps spitting blood due to a rap on the head, plus a busted right ankle. My mate was lying beside the gun platform, his head missing.

By this time the ship was down by the head; looking at the funnel I could see the carnage of what had been the bridge nigh on the funnel, with bodies and body parts lying about the funnel deck. I was numb with shock, stupefied. I hung there like a zombie for God knows how long, then I heard a shout from below to abandon ship so I managed to get to my feet and made my way to the after gun deck. Then I heard a shout, 'slip that raft'! After a struggle and with help of another bod we launched it. I made my way down a ladder to the main deck where I was ordered over the side (not before blowing up my lifebelt), I hit the water and found myself swimming in diesel oil and got a gutful of same. I finally slithered onto the raft that I had helped to release earlier. Quite a few bods were on that raft, I'd hazard a guess about 12 or 14. All I know is there were bods piled on the raft and an odd one or two hanging on to the lifelines, Between others trying to get onboard and a fair swell running it became inevitable that the raft would capsize, which it eventually did.

We had drifted about two or three hundred yards from the ship when suddenly we saw the water between the ship and us was afire and it was gaining on us! Let you understand, seeing from near zero level, distance is hard to judge. Our concern was it was creeping up on us too bloody fast. I saw two bodies with arms flailing swallowed up in the flames, which all added up to our own plight. Here we were, soaked in diesel oil like a lamp wick ready for a light to be applied. I'd the impression that one or two were on the verge of giving up, then for some unknown reason the raft pitched over throwing us over and under, whether through being overloaded, the swell, or shifting bodies is anyone's guess. However I remember going under then grabbing a pair of thrashing legs and pulling myself to the surface, I grabbed a lifeline on the raft and hung on for a time; then, God knows how I did it, I managed to pull myself into the raft. I noticed right away that there was a drastic reduction in the number of bodies, they had just floated away, whether through shock, cold or wounds one will never know.

Those of us remaining were fighting for survival. We were shivering with cold and shock, yet at the same time I can recall the terror of watching those flames creeping closer. One can't put the pace of time on events while in such a situation; to me it seemed a helluva long time. Then, as if by an answer to my prayers, this Russian Sub-chaser (like an MTB) appeared alongside, then two Russian sailors yanked me on board and guided me through a hatch to a warm mess. It was heaven. I sat at a table as a few more joined me and I recall a Russian bringing my attention to a chap laying on a bunk at my back dressed in Tiffy's gear. It was obvious the poor chap was dead. Unfortunately I couldn't put a name to him, but my mind was being distracted with the enormity of events and what might lay ahead. We heard and felt the surge of power of the boat's engines and I knew then they had picked all the bods they could find, - a pathetic few. I can't say for sure how many were picked up.

The Russian sailors did us proud; they even passed round a mug of vodka of which yours truly had a Gulper, no, not a Sipper. While on the subject of Sippers, the 28th of April was my 20th birthday, so you know the age-old custom amongst messmates when the grog's served out in the mess, the lad whose birthday it is generally has a Sipper from his Oppo's tot. I had that but kept a couple of Sippers for the following day the 29th! So between my tot, Sippers and now vodka and diesel, some cocktail!! As I mentioned, I lost all sense of time and so it was with my fellow mates, all bruised and battered but thankfully we'd made it.

We came alongside a jetty at Vaenga and disembarked. We were wrapped in blankets, some walked, two or three stretchered and transported to hospital, there we were allocated to our beds after our injuries had been assessed. I was fortunate; my right ankle was badly swollen, minus a fair patch of skin, flesh and a chipped bone but otherwise fine apart from stinking from diesel oil. My skin took on a yellow hue which remained on me for weeks and the smell of the stuff for days. I was issued with army gear complete with a Russian style furry hat. We were certainly an odd-looking lot.

We heard about VE Day through the hospital staff and I remember thinking how awful for those shipmates who didn't make it, a matter of days before the end of hostilities. We passed time in hospital (those of us that were fit) by reading etc, although I did go out to the local Telegraph Office after bartering fags for roubles and sent a wire to my mother, saying 'safe and well hope to see you soon'. I have it somewhere in my box of memorabilia, a bit jaded but nice to recall my stay in Vaenga.

I teamed up with Alfie Crouch who came through the same experience as myself on the raft. One day he and I were detailed to pick up stores by lorry and in a far corner I came across a pile of kegs of rum. I can't remember the outcome but there were a few pulses racing away in the ward! By the way that hospital was run by RN personnel and no doubt had seen many seamen through its wards, both Royal and Merchant Navies during the Arctic runs as our own situation. As stated earlier it all happened so long ago that I haven't a clue as regards times and dates.

Came a day when those of us that were sound in body were transported down to the docks in Vaenga and there we joined the care and maintenance crew of the destroyer HMS *Cassandra*. She'd had 42 feet of her bows blown off the previous December. A bod told me that when she had docked, there were hammocks still slung with bodies still in them as if asleep. There she was with a bow of sorts fitted to her like a Thames barge when one viewed it from the inside, just nothing except a beam here and there to shore it up. A few of us were a little apprehensive at the prospects of facing the long haul back to the UK as you know the reputation of these waters. In fact we had a helluva battering on the way up. However, we set sail and had an uneventful voyage, arriving at Rosyth Docks, then train to my depot Chatham Barracks (of which there is no more).

Goodall was a happy ship. I was Tanky on her; the beef I had in the fridge was blocks of Irish beef which you thawed in the 'fridge flat'. It was pot luck what was in the block. If I had been on my normal duties that day I would have been blown to pieces. There were many laughs and much comradeship amongst the crew as a whole. We let our hair down whenever we hit port, whether it was in Bootle, Derry etc. I remember one high jinks while tied up in Bootle Dock, before 'Colours'. A matelot had hoisted a pair of WRNS bloomers up the jackstaff. You can imagine the grins of those who saw *Goodall*'s 'conquest' fluttering there amongst the rest of the ships.

We also had our solemn days like Captain Walker's funeral and the loss of our 'chummy' sister ship HMS *Bullen* off Cape Wrath. Time to close the hatch now.

Author's Note
HMS Bullen *was torpedoed on 6th December 1944.*
HMS Cassandra *was torpedoed on 11th December 1944.*

Seaman Torpedoman Cliff Russell
When I first joined *Goodall* I was told that the nickname for the Captain was Bombhead, which came from the following. It was said they were on convoy duty to Gibraltar when they had a radar contact of four to five ships. As you probably know, if it had been a British ship it would give a signal back which would be the victory sign. but this did not happen. So he left the convoy steaming towards this group with the intention of engaging them. Fortunately they turned out to be Canadian destroyers! The other reason for the nickname, his

size in headgear was seventeen and a half inches.

The day we were torpedoed in the Kola Inlet we had abandoned ship and were on a Carley float drifting towards the diesel oil which was alight. Before the fire swallowed us up, luckily we were rescued by a Russian MTB. In the hospital in Russia one lad collected as much of our Russian money as he could get together and went over to the Russian army camp to buy a bottle of vodka. When he got back to the hospital and opened it, found instead of vodka it had been refilled with water and he was raving. What he was going to do to the Russians was nobody's business and he set off back to the camp again but came running back with bullets flying over his head.

When the ship was torpedoed my pal Ted Goss was alongside the Skipper and finished up with his left leg crushed and his left arm smashed in several places. The Skipper was never found. It was not long before gangrene set in and it was decided to amputate the leg. In this hospital in Russia it seems only officers were allowed to have an anaesthetic, so they poured rum down his throat. In his words, he had more rum than blood in his veins when they amputated his leg. I went to see him next morning and there he was sat up in bed with the wireless going, beating time to the music with the stump of his leg.

At one time on exercises while on the depth-charges, the young midshipman was instructed to press the alarm button three times as the signal to drop one depth-charge with a low setting to blow up an imaginary torpedo following the ship. The young midshipman with perhaps a shaky finger and maybe a harder than expected button to press ended up with six notes of the alarm sounding, so I rang the bridge. Told them I did not understand the signal I received and was told in no uncertain terms to 'drop that ruddy depth-charge', so I did. The ship had by now lost speed; the depth-charge exploded at its shallow setting almost underneath us and nearly blew the stern off! Most of the pots, pans and crocks in the after messes finished up on the messdecks in pieces and yours truly was in trouble, of course.

To end with a sad story; when we were in Liverpool for one of our refuelling visits, we were asked if any of the ratings would like to take part in a diving course. It was one of the type using a fully waterproof suit, lead-soled boots and helmet complete with air pipes. After instruction they took their first dive into the dock just behind a ship tied alongside. Tragically, something went wrong, as the ship moved forward snapping the wire 'spring' which shot around cutting through the air pipe supplying one of the divers and he died. I am not sure whether he was one of our ship's company or not.

Stoker E.N. Setchell C/KX 99285

Nelson Setchell was one of the advance party for *Goodall*. He survived the loss of the ship and can be picked out in the group of survivors in a photograph taken of them on the flight deck of HMS *Vindex*.

He wrote the following letter to a Mr Slade who was kind enough to send a copy in reply to my plea for information. It runs as follows: In 1943 after diesel training and related electrics at Roedean girl's school and also at St. Dunstans school for the blind, I then left for America on *Louis Pasteur* (a French liner), arrived at Newport News, Virginia, then on by train to Ashbury Park, New Jersey, then to Boston. We stayed in a converted wool warehouse while the ship was being built. I believe the ship was commissioned in the October when the rest of the crew were there. Started working-up trials (bedding the crew in) which included going to Hamilton, Bermuda and if my memory serves me right we then left Boston early in 1944 for Halifax, Nova Scotia with a convoy to Belfast, Ireland. Here the ship was converted from American canteen messing to British style. Extra depth-charge racks were fitted, Other work was also carried out and after completion we went on to Liverpool to be assigned to the 19th Escort group.

My memory of the Russian run, the Captain's last order was 'stand by to attack' and the rest is history. I can only remember being picked up by a whaler, then *Farnham Castle* coming alongside, hanging on to a 'Jacob's ladder' and then being pulled aboard. After that my mind is a blank, with the next thing I knew I was being on *Vindex* and I believe having a good trip to Scapa. Then down to Chatham, home for 14 days survivor's leave and VE Day. Only other thing I can remember clearly concerns a watch normally allowed £1 if you had lost it with your ship, but I claimed £5 having bought it in Cape Town (after losing two previously). After going through all the channels saw the top brass in Chatham Barracks and I saw more gold braid that day than I had seen all the war (typical 'Barrack Stanchions', Battle of Jutland variety).One question they asked and I can always remember was 'Why, rating do you require a watch?' I nearly replied 'to tell the time', but said instead 'so I would not be late off leave' and got my £5.

Didn't last long in barracks and was drafted to Rosyth in Scotland and demobbed in April 1946.

Author's note

Sad to say Nelson Setchell 'crossed the bar' some years back. He was one of the lucky survivors who fought through the war, serving on other ships before escaping with his life from the carnage of Goodall.

Louis Pasteur was a pre-war French Liner which was one of several large liners taken over and used as troop carriers ferrying troops and personnel around the world. They were fast ships and in many cases, especially on the North Atlantic run, by using the Zig-zag technique combined with their speed would do without an escort once they were clear of the U-boat packs around the UK. When leaving or entering North West approaches, though, it was usual to have two fast destroyers as escorts.

David Parker, Nelson Setchell's son-in-law, has been in touch with me and has donated one of the HMS Goodall *photographs for use in this book.*

There were several others we know who survived and my thanks to David Slade of Billingshurst who in response to my plea in Navy News sent the following:

Alfie Crouch had his action station on 'X' gun at the stern of HMS *Goodall*. He had been wounded in the shoulder and after the torpedo struck went around setting stern depth charges to 'safe', then went into the water before getting onto a Carley float. With him was another A/B, 'Shiner' Wright from Norfolk. Alfie went on to say they were on this for about three hours before being rescued by a Russian MTB. He said there were originally seven in the beginning and recalls:

LTO Bowles (subsequently died of wounds); Laundryman Clare; A/B Lockyer; P/O Prince Albert Consort (not a name to forget) had both arms broken; a South African Officer, had a neck injury.

Arthur Carfoot's action station was in the engine room on the control board; he also managed to get on the same float.

Alongside him in the engine room had been his stoker Fred Howkins and when the torpedo struck everything went dead. It was every man for himself and Arthur managed to get out, into the sea and on the Carley float, but Fred wasn't so lucky. Arthur recalled that Fred Howkins was a gardener by trade and remembered him singing 'roaming in the gloaming' at one of the 'Sods Operas' on board ship. They were landed and treated at Vaenga Hospital, were three months there all suffering from wounds and frostbite.

Lieutenant R.B. Whyte

The following was sent by Robert Wilson, his nephew, about the uncle he never knew.

Robert Reah Whyte, known by his Navy friends and shipmates as 'Knocker', was born in Canada in 1915 while his family was on a posting from England for his father's firm. In 1928/29 the family moved back to England and he had the benefit of an education at Cambridge. He joined the RNVR in 1940, commencing his training as an Ordinary Seaman HO at *Ganges* and went on from there through several shore bases and ships and up through the ranks from SubLieutenant to Lieutenant, eventually joining *Goodall* in February 1944. His role on board was Forecastle Officer and also as Signals Officer involved with coding and ciphers along with the Navigating Officer Geoff Hadden. There seems little doubt that he was on or near the bridge when the torpedo struck and that survivors in or near that area were few and far between. Those who did survive were badly injured.

Robert Wilson, when asked how he became involved, replied that he was seated at his computer and for no reason that he can explain typed in the word *Goodall* and HMS *Goodall* became part of his family history. It soon became a great new interest for him but sadly little of his uncle's life had been recorded by either family (as very often happens, I am afraid). As he researched he found that Russia and the Arctic featured a great deal in his uncle's life. Even pre-war found him on Viking, a four-masted barque and prior to joining *Goodall* was on the trawler HMS *Lord Austin* escorting convoys to Russia. So I suppose it was no surprise to hear that he volunteered to stay with *Goodall* for this Russian convoy even though he should have been drafted off because his posting had come through.

There is a lot more to this story but time and space do not permit. To have survived all through the war only to be killed within days of it ending is nothing else but tragic. There is a similarity here with Michael Rawlinson who lost the father he never knew. It does both of them credit that they have carried out considerable research into something that must have been completely unknown and I suppose even foreign to them because neither Michael or Robert had any experience of WW2. They were then hooked on what became their family research. Both of them have told me they have made many new friends during their research and have felt proud to attend various reunions, functions etc. over the years as they became more involved.

The Rescuers

Accounts from crew members of HMS Anguilla, *HMS* Honeysuckle *and HMS* Loch Insh

HMS Anguilla

Leading Seaman L. Conlon (LTO)

I remember being on the fo'csle at the time *Goodall* was attacked and, being at action station, I was in charge of 'hedgehog' and saw what appeared to be a destroyer hit and the ship's company scrambling about the upper decks.

It is hard to describe one's feelings properly, but I looked across the waves and thought to myself 'God help them', but it was only momentary because I had plenty to occupy myself with along with my shipmates.

I served from 1938 to October 1945 on HMSs *Forester, Belfast* and others as well as *Anguilla*. The real information comes out after the event. At the time after *Goodall* had been hit I would have been following instructions from the bridge regarding the target (U968) which would have been the range, then the order to fire followed by 'Be alert' and 'Ready'.

I think the convoy was probably the last wartime Arctic run and *Goodall* the last major RN ship lost in the war. Only a few days previously we had had a soccer match ashore with them. The best and easiest memories come back when the good times afloat and ashore are recalled and the bad times are pushed out of the memory and are not so easily remembered.

Author's note

A photocopy of a photograph of the soccer team was included in Laurie Conlon's letter, also a photocopy of his 'station card' noting Mess 4, Fo/csle, 1st St'bd, Red Watch and i/c Hedgehog, etc.

Leading Seaman G.W. Redhead P/JX296540

I remember the day well. It was a bright sunny morning, the Flotilla Commander came aboard for the church service. He explained to us that the U-boats were waiting for us to go out so we should know what to expect. He said his ship would be the first out (I can't remember which ship he was on); *Anguilla* would follow and the convoy would assemble.

The next morning the action started straight away. *Goodall* and

Anguilla got a sounding on a U-boat and went in for the attack. Anguilla followed *Goodall* in and was on her starboard quarter when the torpedo struck *Goodall* causing severe damage forward. During the action that followed, U-286 was sunk by *Anguilla* and *Cotton* with *Loch Shin*; U-307 was sunk by *Cygnet*, *Loch Insh* and *Loch Shin*. U-968 fired the torpedo which struck *Goodall* and *Anguilla* had to return later to *Goodall* to carry out the 'Coup de Grace'.

When we rendered the 'Coup de Grace' some fragments from *Goodall* landed on *Anguilla* and while diving for cover one of our officers was not quite quick enough, was struck on the backside and spent the trip back home to UK. lying face down!

HMS *Honeysuckle*

Terry Guest

I was a seventeen and a half year old rating on HMS. *Honeysuckle* K27. On 29th April 1945 we were in the Kola Inlet and I was terrified at the time with all that was happening and now I am trying to remember details from 57 years ago and having to rely on a fading memory .

We on *Honeysuckle* heard the explosion and our ship seemed to fall silent. I was only a youngster but I read the worry and strain on the faces of my older shipmates. It was war at sea in the Arctic. Steaming towards *Goodall* we quickly lowered the seaboat (which incidentally capsized later when it had picked up survivors) we hove to very briefly, went along *Goodall's* starboard side to be able to take aboard the remaining crew and wounded, then went to the assistance of men on the floatnet. Time was critical as the fuel on the sea was alight and had almost reached the net, the flames in fact were coming up our portside as we were picking them up. There were others nearby in the water who we also managed to rescue before the flames reached them and by now Russian MTBs had arrived and I saw a Castle class corvette approaching.

My Captain, Lt. Cdr Wright and the 1st Lieutenant. told me to go below where I helped to clean oil off the survivors and to give 'Kye' to those able to drink. The warmest place I think that day on *Honeysuckle* was in the engine room. There was so much happening at once and at top speed it is difficult to recall everything but I can remember the bow of *Goodall* was gone completely and ammo was flying all over the place; with the thick smoke and dark red flames it was like a scene from hell that words cannot describe. I could hear the escaping steam screaming which filled my head with sound.

H L Mobbs, HMS Honeysuckle. (Crew member of the seaboat lowered to rescue survivors of Goodall.)

The seaboat's crew were: John Strickleton, 'Robbie' Robinson and myself. Another name springs to mind, G. Sharp (although I am not 100% on that one). If I am right, one more name is missing; I wish I knew for certain who he was! At that time our only objective was to save as many of *Goodall's* crew as possible, but as you can see by the print of my painting we were overwhelmed, which was not surprising. I hoped they made it to *Farnham Castle* which was not too far away. A raft near the oil had two men on it and I have often wondered whether they survived or not.

The print shows *Honysuckle* going forward of *Goodall* having previously stemmed (rammed) her stem into the stern of *Goodall* to be able to take off injured survivors. The sea in fact was choppier than I have shown.

Author's note

Elsewhere it is noted that the seaboat was overturned just as it was preparing to disembark the survivors they had rescued. Len hoped they had all been lucky enough to have reached safety and hoped the same for the two in the raft. He was of course fighting for his own survival at that time.

Also it is worth pointing out for the benefit of readers not in the RN of those days that the seaboat was propelled by oars, not a motor.

'Lennie' Mobbs is an accomplished artist of marine paintings and I understand his paintings can be seen at many reunions.

Leading Seaman Eric G (Robbie) Robinson

I served five years in *Honeysuckle* 1940-1945 but the last war-time convoy to Murmansk proved to be the worst from my point of view as it nearly cost me my life.

The last ship sunk in the European War was the frigate HMS *Goodall*. It was 'fished' on April 29th. 1945. She was hit in her forward magazine and all her fo'scle was blown away right back to her bridge, her deck was curled back like a sardine can lid. *Honeysuckle* was quite 'close to' and went over to give assistance, *Goodall* was a raging inferno inside; her sides were cherry-red with the heat and turning the sea water into steam. We were unable to go alongside under these conditions so our Skipper rammed our bows into her square stern which caused two holes in our bows but had the effect of locking the two ships together. Sub-Lt Bell (a New Zealander) and some more of our crew jumped across aboard *Goodall* and rescued some of the engineers.

At this point, I went off with my lads in the 'Port' sea-boat to pick up men who were in the water; collecting quite a number, maybe more than I should have done considering the size of the boat, because at that time we were pretty well down in the water. In the meantime diesel fuel was pouring out of *Goodall* and spreading all over the surface of the sea. Somewhere it came in contact with a calcium flare and Boom, the sea was ablaze and our sea-boat was surrounded by flames. There was no opening anywhere and I was wondering how we were going to get out of this right old mess; there was just no place to go. I shudder to think of what might have happened had the frigate *Farnham Castle* not turned up to our rescue.

Looking like a fire-tender she came through the flames with all her fire hoses blasting the burning fuel out of her path, She was so close when she came through the flames that she almost ran us down. She had a fair amount of way on her and when a line was thrown and caught, my boat was towed under and capsized; now everyone was in the water! The sea temperature, as you may well guess, was low enough to totally incapacitate the proverbial metallic primate and the shock of being immersed in that almost knocked you unconscious. I thought my number was up this time, for I was all dressed up in winter-clothing etc with my lovely well-fitting seaboots on, too.

I couldn't kick them off, so together with all the other added weight I went down and down and down. I thought it was getting somewhat dark down there so I made a desperate effort and forced myself back up to the surface and daylight. I managed to catch .a heaving line thrown to me, but my frozen hands could not hold it and it was pulled out of my non-existent grasp. The 'well-fitting leather seaboots' took charge once more and attempted to take me down to Davy Jones Locker. Next time I surfaced I shouted to the matelot who threw the line to let it slacken when I caught it so I could wrap it around my waist, he did and I survived. My boat's crew survived too, but I think some of the men I had picked up didn't. Two helpings of that sort of thing never did anybody any good at all.

Late in the evening, my crew and I were taken aboard a Russian MGB that took us back to *Honeysuckle*. She didn't look too good either, with two holes in her bows, and scorched, blackened and blistered paintwork, she looked a bit 'burnt up'.

We arrived back in the Clyde on VE Day, May 8th 1945.

HMS Loch Insh

Omri Jones, Coder

HMS *Goodall* was sunk (torpedoed) at 1930 hrs. on Sunday 29th.
April 1945. I was standing on the port side aft of Loch Insh, not more
than fifty or sixty yards in direct line with *Goodall*. There was a loud
explosion, the aerials and mast were dislodged and fell backwards
into the bridge and funnels. The superstructure seemed to be a
complete mess and men were in the very cold water. We were busy
picking up survivors from U-307 I believe. Although most of the
escort vessels were unknown to us, HMSs *Zephyr* and *Zealous* were
steaming parallel on the starboard side. I had the knowledge in my
job that at least ten U-boats were waiting for us at the entrance to the
Kola Inlet, though possibly few survived ?

I subsequently found the name of a colleague of mine who was on
Goodall in the list of those lost, so sadly he was not one of the
survivors.

Each Armistice Day I remember this incident vividly, not at all
pleasant.

John Roberts

Our main task was anti-submarine patrols lasting three weeks or
longer and often we used to tie up alongside *Goodall* when we
entered Gladstone Dock, Liverpool for a boiler clean.

In April 1945 we were ordered to Scapa Flow to escort a convoy
to Russia. We left Scapa in company with HMSs *Cotton, Anguilla* and
Loch Shin; also there were *Vindex* and *Bellona*. The outward trip was
uneventful and although there were plenty of alarms and action
stations, we arrived without any losses. The convoy went on to
Archangel while we, the escort group, tied up at Vaenga. *Loch Insh*
tied up beneath the signal station where we stayed another week or
so alongside two Russian destroyers.

On 29th April at about 1600 hours it was piped 'clear lower deck
muster on the quarterdeck.' The skipper, Lt-Cdr.E.Dempster, gave us
the details of the return convoy RA66. We were to sweep ahead of the
convoy so we were the first ship out. He explained we were to cross
a minefield and there were also 13 U-boats out there waiting for us.
On the way across the Kola Inlet we narrowly missed a mine that the
masthead lookout spotted and we steered clear of it.

I shall never forget that night and recall that 'hands to supper' had
just been piped. We had started dishing up egg, chips and, tomatoes

and I was just about to spear a chip when 'action stations' was sounded about 1910 hours. As I closed up to the starboard twin Oerlikon I could see about three to four hundred yards on the starboard beam *Goodall* on fire with the forepart crumpled right up to the bridge. Black smoke and flames were pouring from her with the sea around also on fire. Then I noticed a number of MLs or rescue boats coming to assist with rescuing survivors. Almost at once we had an ASDIC contact and carrying out an antisub attack we fired a pattern of 'squid' which blew U-307 to the surface. We opened fire with all weapons; the first shell missed but discernable through the black smoke and we continued dropping charges.

I think we sank U-286 but this was not the one that torpedoed *Goodall* although we did not know at the time. *Honeysuckle* went alongside to rescue survivors and she stayed long enough for her paintwork to catch fire, so they had to leave for their own safety. I remember I had the middle watch as quartermaster, during which I heard a lot of gunfire which must have been when the remains of *Goodall* were sunk. I believe the official jargon would have been (dispatched by our own forces).

I remember wondering at that time if the Canteen Manager aboard *Goodall* had been saved as he, PO Alec Brown, was my next door neighbour. What could I say to his wife, that is if he did not survive and we ourselves managed to get back safely. As it happened fortunately he was saved, although I did not know this until much later, in fact not until I returned from the Far East in 1947 and found that he had spent six months in Vaenga before getting home.

On our way back home with the convoy to UK, peace was declared and we went to Leith for a refit, where we also landed the survivors from the U-boat. Then we sailed for the Far East.

Author's Note

It seems possible that the Canteen Manager came home on the Fleet Carrier HMS Queen *and was among the patients named as* Goodall *survivors in the sick bay.*

NAVY ABBREVIATIONS & SLANG

All Navy and ex-Navy readers will, of course, be fully aware of the meaning of the following expressions which occur in this book, but they are included for the benefit of those who did not enjoy the benefits of naval service.

Andrew = Royal Navy. The name is said to have been that of an 18th-century Lieutenant, notorious for his expert leadership of a pressgang.

Buzz = rumour

French letter = A now politically incorrect name for a condom. (The French retaliated by calling it *une capote anglaise.* (English coat))

Green rub = a raw deal

H.O. =(Hostilities Only)

Jimmy = the First Lieutenant

Kye = A hot drink, the principal constituents of which are cocoa, sugar and rum.

SBA = Sick Berth Attendant.

Sippers/Gulpers. Both these expressions refer to the amount of grog to be taken from a mate's 'tot' of rum when invited to do so for celebratory purposes, e.g, birthday, promotion and so forth.

Sprog = New recruit.

Tiffy's gear = the uniform worn by personnel of the non-seaman branch i.e. steward, stores assistant, etc.

War service of HMS Goodall K479

October 1943 - April 1945

04.10.43	Commissioned BOSTON (USA).
13.11.43	To CASCO BAY, PORTLAND (MAINE, USA) for gunnery & Depth-charge exercises. (HMS *Bullen* in company).
02.12.43	To BERMUDA for working-up exercises. (HMS *Bullen* in company).
26.12.43	To BOSTON (USA) for engine repairs.
31.12.43	To BELFAST (Pollock Dock) for refitting. (HMS *Aylmer* in company).
31.01.44	Escorting Convoy ON228 to ST JOHN'S, NEWFOUNDLAND. (B6 Escort Group and HMS *Swale* in company).
17.03.44	Aircraft 210 to investigate echoes.
18.03.44	U-Boat detected bearing 270, 30 miles.
05.04.44	Chasing echoes. (HMS *Bentley* in company).
13.04.44	Returned LIVERPOOL. Many encounters with ice packs on voyage. Transferred to CLYDE as independent unit.
28.04.44	Escorting SS *Cameronia* to ICELAND and back. (HMS *Bullen* in company).
22.05.44	Patrolling to 30 West. Returned to BELFAST.
05.06.44	Using codename CROFTER, preparing for D-Day. (HMS *Duncan* in company, codename OAKOVER).
06.06.44	Escorting HMS *Nelson* to Normandy coast, 10 nautical miles East of CHERBOURG. (HMS *Bullen* in company). Returned to PLYMOUTH.
08.06.44	To LIVERPOOL.
10.06.44	Patrolling BLOODY FORELAND to SLYNE HEAD.(HMSs *Bulldog*, *Bullen* and *Duncan* in company). Sighted Focke-Wulf 200K, also FAA Swordfish.
16.06.44	Sub echo close.
24.06.44	To CLYDE escorting SS *Highland Princess*. (HMS *Bullen* in company} Submarine contact 55.52'N,09.11' W, later at 56.11' N, 7.40'W.
01.07.44	In company with Escort Carrier HMS *Vindex* and HMS

	Manners on anti-submarine patrol MINCHES and TIREE. ROCKALL also included in search area aided by Sunderland flying boat. On return, stopped & searched fishing trawler.
14.07.44	To CLYDE for Compass tests.
26.07.44	To ICELAND, escorting SS *Otranto*. (HMS *Bullen* in company).
07.08.44	Exercise with HM Submarine *Seraph*.
10.08.44	Escorted convoy to Gibraltar, arriving 17.08.44.
06.09.44	Return to UK. Attacked submarine off LUNDY ISLAND, 51.27' N, 4.33' W., D/C 22 fathoms. 'Kill' not certain.
07.09.44	To BELFAST for fitting of anti-cavitation device.
17.09.44	To CLYDE (LARGS & FAIRLIE RANGE) with HM Submarine *Seraph*.19th Escort Group formed. Commenced working-up with *Hesperus, Bullen, Loch Insh, Antigua, Anguilla*.
16.10.44	CLYDE with 19 Escort Group.
03.11.44	Searching SOUTH COAST for six LCTs swamped in heavy seas. Returned to HOLYHEAD after calibration and exercises with HM Submarine *Seraph*.
12.11.44	To LIVERPOOL, thence to CLYDE, LOCH EWE, DUNNETT HEAD, BUTT of LEWIS, STORNOWAY, TIUMPAN HEAD, SHIANT ISLES, carrying out anti-submarine sweeps.
06.12.44	HMS *Bullen* torpedoed 7 miles N of CAPE WRATH. During the following 36-hour search, HMSs *Goodall* and *Loch Insh* claimed the sinking of U-297. RAF Coastal Command made a similar claim after an attack by a Sunderland flying boat.
26.12.44	To ENGLISH CHANNEL with Group seeking 2-man submarines inside 5-fathom line for a month.
28.01.45	To LIVERPOOL, where the compiler of this log, Sub-Lieutenant Paul Mallet, was transferred from *Goodall*.

The remainder of HMS *Goodall's* short life was spent, in company with the other ships of 19th Escort Group on escort duty for the merchant vessels carrying vital supplies to the Russian Arctic port of Murmansk, during which, as this book relates, she met her fate on 29th April 1945. After having travelled some 53000 nautical miles on His Majesty's service she became the last RN ship to be sunk during the war in Europe.